I0380262

Adelaide: Mapping the Human City

Adelaide: Mapping the Human City

Edited by Deb Stewart

For the City of Adelaide, its people and its visitors
(the capital city of South Australia)
34° 55' S, 138° 35' E

Adelaide: Mapping the Human City
ISBN 978 1 76109 141 4
Copyright © poems individual contributors 2021
Copyright © this collection Deb Stewart 2021
Cover image: Deb Stewart 2020

First published 2021 by
GINNINDERRA PRESS
PO Box 3461 Port Adelaide 5015 Australia
www.ginninderrapress.com.au

Contents

Elder Park Rotunda, 2020 (Deb Stewart)

Introduction

Adelaide has, at one time or another, been home to most, if not all, of the poets included in this anthology. For those who might wonder where in the universe it is, Adelaide (the capital city of South Australia) is situated on the Adelaide Plains at 34° 55' S, 138° 35' E with the coast to its west and the Mount Lofty Ranges to its east. The city is laid out as a grid of streets surrounded by parklands, with a paved mall – Rundle Mall – and five public squares. The central square, Victoria Square/Tarntanyangga, isn't really a square at all but closer to a rectangle dissected by a diamond configuration of roadways.

North Adelaide is a series of smaller grids two to three kilometres from the CBD, also surrounded by parklands, with its own public square – Wellington Square – and set at a bit of an angle in relation to the city.

I invited some local poets to contribute to this introduction by describing Adelaide in a couple of short sentences and their responses, combined below, capture many of the city's characteristics.

Adelaide is at once a place of worship and dark secrets, camouflaged by pretty trees. Once known as the City of Churches, Adelaide has grown to worship art, theatre, live music, literature, spoken word, and, curiously, football. A broad church indeed.

It is also thought to be a sleepy town with a dark undercurrent but is really a place of close encounters under plane trees, jacaranda and wisteria. A city that defends its soul along with the trees that line its streets, although livelier than many realise and friendlier than many expect.

Similar to the Tadpole Galaxy,* but with a greater socio-economic divide; the local variety of pub-dwellers are more sentimental, and the bull ants are fiercer. Something to savour in Adelaide is a fabulous Balfours pie, perhaps from the old pie cart outside the railway station on North Terrace, turned upside down and floating in a thick sea of pea soup with a blob of tomato or Worcestershire sauce on top. Or served with chips at the Balfours Café, followed with a green or pink iced frog cake.

Adelaide is a modestly sized, vibrantly diverse and picturesque city abundant with hidden gastronomical gems, the spirit of many cultures, live entertainment and recreational activities. It is the pulsating artery of the festival state, feeding its inhabitants with wine, wonders, whimsy and meals for clusters of kerbside pigeons. A meeting place of many minds, café nooks to caffeinate and pass the time. On each street corner lies something bewitching: verdant trees, a melange of architecture, a confluence of crowds and venous alleyways. Everything beautiful, being, belonging, and its sprawling parklands are pockets of quietude in frenzied urban sublime.

Adelaide is a comforting city, planned on a square, surrounded by green parks, trees and mellowed old buildings. The best city for clean air and sociable living.

The poems in this anthology are alive with many of the characteristics described above.

This may be the first full-length poetry anthology set entirely in the city of Adelaide. If one has been published before,

* Contributors to this introduction were asked how they would describe Adelaide to visitors from outer space.

I was not able to locate it, although there appear to have been a few short individual collections published over the years, notably Amelia Walker's *Fat Streets & Lots of Squares* (2003) and Richard Tipping's *Tommy Ruff: Adelaide Poems* (2014). A collection titled *Adelaide sonnets: a biography of the city* by Peter Bladen was published around 1975, while two collections written in Adelaide, but perhaps not about Adelaide, are *Adelaide lunch sonnets* by Thomas Shapcott (2006) and *At the Flash and At the Baci* by Ken Bolton (2006). Jeff Guess has written several poems about, or set in, Adelaide and many of these were included in an exhibition – *Dream Houses – Adelaide in Poems and Pictures* – at David Jones in Adelaide, 1990.

The initial idea for this collection of poetry came from my attendance at the Literary Adelaide symposium, University of Adelaide, in 2012, and the call for submissions went out as I was preparing to run a series of workshops on writing poetry about Adelaide as Poet-in-Residence at the City Library, early in 2020. The collection contains a few collaborative poems written during one of these workshops.

There are close to a hundred poems by over sixty poets who will take you all over the city – from Elder Park to Whitmore Square, Rundle Mall to South Terrace, the Botanic Gardens to North Adelaide and many places in between.

Deb Stewart

With thanks to Pam Makin, Sarah Jane Justice, Jen Allen, Bethany Cody, Val Smith and Tess Driver for their contributions to this introduction.

Adelaide, South Australia

This is the country where daphne and gardenia will not grow: here on the alkaline soil of the plains that flatten out like supplicants at prayer before the high-rise of the hills where a poet said 'the future stops': the hills which showcase the seasons like window displays in the mall: fog in winter and fire in summer; where Japanese maples glow in autumn as they were meant to and gardeners, unbridled as conspicuous consumers, plant azalea and camellia without restraint.

This is the country where almond and olive shoot like weeds; where daphne grows in pots of acidic soil and gardenia is kept under glass against nights as cold as the desert sand.

This is the country of furry-skinned fruit whose stone hearts, if ripening late, set hard, free of flesh bled dry of juice. The soft flesh and sweet liquid of early ripeners is soon a memory. This is the country where black seed and soft skin travel as tourists.

This is the country of rain that spits; rain so rare, so short in duration it's easy to miss. People complain about regular rain; they think of crisis; they have no sense of averages.

This is the country of hardness and salt, of clay, white lakes and balding scrub edging out to broken shell and shard.

This is the country of grids and tracks where the sun sets on the line of the horizon in a light washed of colour that might signal blinding revelation did it not immediately trigger a fluid and easy amnesia.

Moya Costello

alighting

Sky's blue linen tablecloth
covers our city's cartographer
pointing from concrete pulpit.
Tourists' photos seek
to capture Adelaide's
grid of placemats
locked step with hope
of happyness snaps
chemical holders of untold stories.

Michele Saint Yves

Here lies

(Light Square Memorial)

Here lies William aligned
north and south his bones they moulder
east and west of memories marketplace,
and a double portrait eyes dubiously
peering through more plans and clash
of arms, tribes of trigonometry,

and just out of sight, almighty and proud
money for beer and rent-a soul
a pub on every corner, hail fellow well-met
a church on every Sunday,
hallelujah parliament

and in the south-west corner
some statue (no expense spared here) –
also as seen on the five-spot,
and to the north a metal knot,
where a faraway horn sounds
like a flugel…man.

What of the old people now,
Captain Jack and his good wife,
her namesake a grey kangaroo,
but only the stars wheel the same
overhead as ever,
apparently even the grumblers
were ashamed to open
their mouths back then –

so here then,
here lies William,
he was a measure
of the man.

Avalanche

Early Morning Bruegel

In Rundle Street: a grey coated man pushes a trolley full
of lumpy sacks, grumbles at kids who whistle and goad;
down the lane, a urine-stained doorway holds a
sleeping man, newspaper- shielded from passing eyes;
a clump of fluorescent cyclists flashes by; a frenzied
busker, missing a string, repels donors with his filthy
feet and discord; twin toddlers in Shrek ears stare at an
 orange-vested, orange-bearded *Big Issue* vendor, a tall
Sudanese teen wipes Hungry Jack's window clean,
stops to contemplate his reflection, and I wonder, as he
might too, who is it that looks back at us and how did
we come to be in this curious composition?

Jude Aquilina

Adelaide I dream You

after Andrew Zawacki and Sarah Holland Batt

Adelaide I dream you, cream rollers breaking froth
against your weatherworn jetties, your neat and tidy beaches
licked white by the tongue of the southern ocean, beachgoers
sipping on flat whites and lattes, white froth tops swirled
with dark brown hearts, Adelaide I dream your hot December
your Christmas pageant parade, Adelaide, your giant plastic
Santa and your blow-up snowmen, is the fire of the sun
like the snow, Adelaide? do you want to make it so?
Your crinoline-frilled history, your spinning-parasol past,
      with corseted
women in Miss Gladys Sym Choon shoes, photochrome
      postcards
of wide open streets, the dirt beaten flat over what lies
beneath, what are you trying to hide, Adelaide, in your neat
      and tidy
chart? all laid out in a grid, Adelaide, Hindley St at your criss-
crossed heart, the sticky mango-sweet of the Empire shisha,
      the onoffonoff
outlines of empty neon bodies, Crazy Horse strippers in
      garish wigs
gaped at by lads in shirts and ties, the punch and shrill of
      gold-filled pokies
the beer-stained, blood-stained pavements, your dreams are
      turning inside
me, Adelaide, do our outsides reflect our insides or our insides
our outsides? my face is starting to change, Adelaide, I think
I might be you, your hidden pain, your homesick past, the
      slap slap slap

of your northern suburbs, white salt pans and scrubland
      paddocks
factories and flat-packed landscape, your long straight
      highways littered
with billboard warnings, littered with crow-picked roadkill,
      glittered
with cellophaned grief, I don't know if I belong, Adelaide, I
      don't know
if you belong, what does it mean to belong, Adelaide? d'you
      remember
how this began? you act like it's all yours, Adelaide, as if
you'd always been here, swirling your dusty petticoats,
      clattering
curlicued balconies, is forgetting the only solution? the old
me is starting to fade, Adelaide, it's making me afraid, I think
we can fix this, I do Adelaide, but we've still got a lot to learn.

Alison Flett

Rundle Street looking west, 1936
(State Library of South Australia, B9358)

Press me into your Herbarium

I am here amongst the collection
in the air-tight vault
of the State Herbarium.

Through the sage smell,
I sense
the many hands that touched
the once living
now dry lifeless life.
I feel the suspension
of plants, mosses and fungi,
endless days and nights
trapped in jars,
between fine paper
sheets,
with the gas.*

Specimens
in cardboard boxes
aching to see the light.
Flattened into a void
excluding radiant stars,
water and complex soil,
our beginnings.

All these stems and seeds
dried and revived
in the germination of ideas
abilities and conversations
papers and PhDs.

Below the store of ancient DNA.
Studied by scientists
and students
traced by volunteers,
pressing and gluing
an entire organisation together.

I feel for the kelp pulled from wild sea
plants from an ancient earth.
I leave before
this silent place desiccates me.

Shaine Melrose

* Inergen Gas fire suppression system operates in the vault to protect
the specimens.

Loss Botanic

Little knew we, bench-sitting under the overt springtime
    fragrance
Of the wisteria arch, caressed by breezes reaching
Us with coastal energy, applauded by the social chatter of
    fruit bats and
Lit by crepuscular dapples that shone on your beauty with
    the angles of sorcery
In a time that melted around the magnetic clasp of our fingers,

That we'd find ourselves here.

Here, after a summer that has scorched all around
This botanic oasis, with gusts singing and singeing
With gleeful menace, replacing birdsong from vanished trees
With eroded love, misread monosyllables and fortnightly silences.
Here in the cross-eyed crossroad,
Facing the bare, pyrophiliac ground around us.

Breathless both, we face different ways and keep different times.
You hike to peaks while I descend to the shore.
We shed empty platitudes, just as the pines shed their crop of
    bats, harvested as ground rotting fruit.

We realise that when we left the garden the garden left us.

Walter Barbieri

Nelumbo Pond – Botanic Gardens

Oh, glorious Nelumbo pond!
I adore your pink blossoms
so intricately pleated
unfolding their yellow light.
Your bright green leaves
of sunlight and shadow
bringing me joy.
A sea of fresh hope
for the adventures
of a boy on a swan
clasping the bird's long neck
with contented glee
a pair of cut lotus blooms
resting gently at the swan's throat
a summer offering
to make my heart swell
with lotus love.

Deb Stewart

First Kiss

I remember the Adelaide Oval
in the early 1980s.
The welcome of the Victor Richardson Gates,
the charm of the historic, old scoreboard,
the beauty of St Peter's Cathedral,
the soft rub of the grassy mounds,
the seated shade of the Morton Bay figs,
the sensation, of gravelly, cement-filled terraces.

I remember the Adelaide Oval
in the early 1980s.
The welcome of your opening words,
the charm of your young, feminine wiles,
the beauty of innocent longing,
the soft rub of our teenage hands,
the seated shade of the Sir Edwin Smith Stand,
the sensation, of sharing my first-ever kiss.

Brenton Cox

Field of Dreams

The first 'Showdown' at the new Adelaide Oval, Saturday 29 March 2014

In soft autumn sunshine
from a high spiral punt kick
the ball is tumbling down
the leagues of warm air into safe hands.

Messy in the forward lines, Westhoff
stands under it, climbs on his team's
shoulders – takes a 'mark of the day'.
The Sunday Mail has its front page early.

Dangerfield is loose on the wing;
a record crowd pumps up the score.
Five o'clock shadows make giants
of mere mortal men.

Eddie Betts with three goals
in one quarter 'walks on water'.
Commentators 'talk him up'.
Off hands. The siren holds its breath.

This is a 'big day at the office'.
The Crows shift a gear. The
boundary umpire works at overtime.
Dreams of playing in the number 1 guernsey.

Game on. 50,000 on their seat's edge.
Port climb the scales. The crowd
is worth two goals. Crows need to lift.
Chad Wingard kicks into the future.

The Power – home with the sun!

Jeff Guess

Elder Park Rotunda with city buildings in the background, 2020 (Deb Stewart)

Views From Elder Park

shadows of Festival theatre
fall black across grassy banks
the river silver-flecked
curves towards the weir

Popeye stutters to a halt
is rope-tied to bollards
ignored by a pair of ducks
that waddle past the landing stage

pedal boats are confetti dots
full of the giggle of children
legs pushing double time
against the cascade of a fountain

on the adjacent lawns
the rotunda stands
has stood for over a century
a host for brass bands

and a daytime playground
for laughing toddlers
and later when the sun goes down
a romantic tryst for lovers

rowing eights in late afternoon
swish their blades back and forth
drip silver tinsel from their oars
as they head back to the boathouse

on the winding towpath
cyclists perch over handlebars
ride into the glare of sun
as it chromes the water

a swan leads its cygnets
softly into the shallows
the swish of rushes in their wake
loud calls across the river

Jill Gower

River Torrens

Ripples in semi circles
radiate toward the northern bank
A glittering snake slithers into reeds
The roar of cars on King William bridge
smell of cut grass on the beat
cigarette smoke wafts along paths at the water's edge
as *Popeye* cruises slowly downriver to the weir
young children's laughter echoes from the stern
A family picnicking on the bank
is careful to not let the wind catch their paperbags
oblivious to history, feeding the ducks bread
The bodies the river has taken
five young children, Dr George Duncan
so many dead
the stagnant odour of yesterday
hangs like fog on the lake

Ash Stewart

The Adelaide Gaol Seen From the Golf Course

If I were somewhere else
perhaps I'd write about the cold
the snow the utter
stillness the silence
the crystal absences

but the heat here
is neither reflective
nor do I think about
much
what you are doing
while you're not with me

separation I suppose
is weather
neither to be ignored
nor quarreled with

*

Outside the gaol
the purple insurrection of
bougainvillea
creeping with police

and over the warm face
of the dammed river
dragonflies
like grappling helicopters
hover and couple

*

Now there are words moving through the grass
the hot stones of the gaol at mid-morning
glow like sunflowers
the turf
creeps northward with golfers
the river stagnates
grows weed
will begin to smell
in the unseen centre of the gaol
a warder is being chipped from a block of ice

*

You are perhaps now
clearing away the chicken
offering the cheese
your eyes
catch something absent
in the mirror
the warder melts a little into the river
the weeds weave
the dragonflies flit and flirt
the police get uneasy and break their cover

*

Easy enough
the kiddies crawl around the cannon
the word goes out through the grass and burns the wrappings
everything's all cleaned up
the stone wall smiles and smiles
the word that dies at my feet as I beat at the blazing grass
is cold
but that's not the word
the grass
is trying to reach me

*

The gaol is hardly visible
through bougainvillea police the lie of the river
and the intent of the city
golf is merely a way of being hot
coolly
whatever you are doing
even though I've no idea what it is
you're doing it to me

*

Under the greens the lawn beetles are tunnelling
the river stagnates and the old stone
breathes the rest of the heat back
forgetfully
to the bougainvillea

your guests surely have gone home
the kids are slotted into cots
and the gaol sleeps in its fluorescent solitude

the warder has evaporated and the police
settle for the night among olives and grevilleas
they are hot and very uncomfortable

I wish I could send them a message of ice
they could test it on their tongues

instead
I'm sending you a portrait of the Adelaide gaol
seen from the inside
of a hot night
and solitary

Andrew Taylor

Adelaide

South Australia

An early morning rower dips his oars
in gold but the ripples spread
and slap in the old black hollows
along the green fringed tidy bank.

The river is dammed –
the old worn profile of a lie
where children fish for their faces
in the green weir's silence.

Tended parklands are a carved ornate
frame that fixes a pretty canvas;
in the gallery – a chamber of horrors
and city walls hang more than pictures.

Lovers in the strip shade of palms
in smooth curve and dips of clover
lie on flat files of unsolved crime –
buried bits of bone between their lips.

There is a tattoo on the parade ground,
the overblown exercise of toy soldiers
that strut into the children's eyes
who afterwards ask to touch the guns.

The Union Jack waves Government House:
beneath the fallen leaves dead drunk
a young man drinks its blended colours
from a long brown paper bag.

The cold cramped floor of the Cathedral
crawls down postcard steps and slips
into the sunbaked street where a woman
scans newspaper 'Births and Deaths'.

Behind her rustic garden seat, plane
trees are keeping something back – death
lurks beneath a blade of grass and
tonight's top TV news – about to happen.

Jeff Guess

The Weir – Changing

from the verse novel – *An Adelaide Boy*

Generations of Adelaide boys
have fished and swum at the Torrens weir.
There's a photo at the State Library
of five boys playing in shallow water
on the other side of the sluice gates
before they were installed.
It's taken in the early 1900s
and the boys are all naked,
without any shame.
Was it different then?
Or did the men with secret desires
always lurk there in bushes and change sheds
awaiting their prey.

One summer I was taken by surprise
in the old stone building – cool, damp
reeking of urine
keeping the shouts of play
at a distance.

Paralysed, I clenched my whole body, aware of my skin
the tug at my swim trunks. Thick fingers trembling
over early pubic hair. The fight or flight response letting me down
as bearded lips brushed me there, thrill of tongue, trembling thighs
a sick chill in my stomach, being drawn in, afraid, confused, but
somehow pleasant, heart lurching, unsure how to move away,
to end. Creak of old wooden door, the slackening of a spider web,
a fly caught in sticky silk, to be devoured. The world of boys bursts in,
innocent, the flick of towels, push and shove of rough play, breaking
the act, in a flurry of escape. Utterly changed.

Deb Stewart

Torrens Weir, 2008 (Deb Stewart)

Adelaide

Vine leaves in the street.
The Mediterranean morning transplanted here,
the Athens of the south, inverted as shadows
are inverted, as seasons are. Meanwhile,
we're a long way from Santorini or Corfu,
Liguria even, or the shipwreck beach of MTV,
of screensavers, of legend. All the classical
destinations. Sails over the street-side tables,
red, Phoenician, filling with morning wind.
We've imported it, this impulse to dine al fresco,
to barter over details, and the old rootstocks
of vine, of culture. A porcelain mug white
as a whitewashed cupola, or blue, sky blue,
as an ocean, as the Aegean.

Thom Sullivan

The Dining Room of the South Australian Hotel*

With glorious sweeping balconies
across from the Adelaide Railway Station,
the three-storey majestic late Victorian era
South Australian Hotel
was a jewel of North Terrace.

Renovated in 1934
sparkling white and gold
with crystal chandeliers,
Louisa O'Brien (the 'Grand Dame' of hotels)
created the finest place to dine
in the entire city.

After pleasantly greeting guests
and acidly scolding staff,
Louisa and her five children
descended the impressive cedar staircase
each evening to take their places in the dining room.

The authoritative head-waiter, Lewy Cotton,
(holding the position for thirty years)
enforced the strict dress code
enquiring whether 'Have we a tie, sir?'
whenever needed.

The list of guests included
H.G. Wells, Anna Pavlova, Marlene Dietrich,
Sir Laurence Olivier, Vivien Leigh, Noel Coward, Katharine Hepburn
and the Beatles.

Rob McKinnon

* The South Australian Hotel was demolished in 1971 and the Ansett
Gateway Hotel (now Stamford Plaza) was built on the site.

Ayers House

Entering through the majestic front doors,
The overwhelming sense of eras past engulfs my being.
The beauty of the costumes,
The elegance of the time,
The knowledge of times past.

Gowns, bonnets and shawls once worn,
Gloves, corsets and silk in handmade excellence.
Walking through the exquisite mansion of Sir Henry Ayers,
With a feeling of being transported back in time.

The peaceful simplicity of an era now gone,
I turn to leave with a glance back.
Admiration flows for the exquisite architecture,
Adelaide's last remaining Grand Mansion.
A step out the door,
Back into the hectic, turbulent present.

Brittany McGorm

The Museum

North Terrace, Adelaide

Animals in glass cases,
birds swooping from ceilings,
skeletons out of cupboards.

Egyptian mummies
wondering where their daddies are,
vases and coins, glass coloured jars.

Insects and other things,
just a bit stuffed,
and mounted on walls,
colourful, distinct.

Vast halls full of natural wonders.
We peer and peek,
love to play hide and seek
in dark corners,
overshadowed by elephants,
whales and dinosaurs.

Bones, dry and brittle,
glued together to make
shapes, to deceive us
into thinking it's prehistoric.

Artefacts, souvenirs.
A museum full of heritage,
history, happenings,
from this wonder world
in which we live.

Airlie Kirkham

The Egyptian Room

The South Australian Museum

Higher up then it all seemed, somewhere above the narrow
dark stairway to the small room our childhood
somehow depended on. Standing on our toes
our noses barely at the glass, we understood

even then and felt the edges of something
difficult – that afterward troubling our dreams we would
not put words to for a long time. Coming
in from the winter's city streets dripping with cold

with mother to this private place, where so many years hung
on the faces of the dead. And in the deep glass cases
of green painted wood, things folded away for so long
still mattered. It was the closest

we had ever come to death.
Knowing little then of even pain. Standing afterwards
somewhere within the warm deep folds of her dress.
Losing later at lunch in Woolworths amidst noise and fuss

things I think I went back to show them yesterday –
on the train, through a wet and winter city.
Clattering up the noisy stone stairway
to the same room, after so many years to see

that nothing had changed, only what I
couldn't hold back. Standing where she once stood
for us, beside King Khafra's cast. Seeing with different eyes
in this small dark old room, crowded

with a class of kids no less absorbed with that strange
spell and sorrow, clutching always at the heart of things.
Here: where it will always be a kind of summer, along
the banks of a green Nile and in the Valley of the Kings.

Jeff Guess

Adelayed Reaction

City of empty churches, chopped
down 'native' trees, raked up
smouldering 'autumn leaves' –
smudge on the satellite photo of
the world's driest state.

Parklands flattened for sport, for
symmetry, for solitude: 1836 you could get lost
in what would be the city square –
Victoria, queen of forgotten maps, excusing deaths,
poisoned flour, disease and bayonets.

Kaurna, the originals, people of the possum skin,
reed basketed, hand axes hidden in the roots of river gums.
Free settlers in bonny striped hats, sweating pioneers
lugging their pianos through the scrub.

On a clear night the hills
rear like a frozen breaker over the iron plain,
huge waves of negativity dampening undue enthusiasm,
the culture burst of the Festival
lighting up the Stony Desert,
crowds of irony spotters banked up like daylight saving
singling out who should be bitched about
for ambiguous behaviour:

all the creeping paralysis of Tiny Town.

And give us this day our *Advertiser,* the only
newspaper in Australia true to its name.

A nice dry northerly blowing topsoil in
until the sky turns brown,
radioactive influence
flowing muddily past the zoo.

Richard Tipping

Parkland Home

she never named the noise she makes
stout, fat sound in racket tones
the cackle she spits from her bill
she knows it only in the sense
that it is hers

she hears the name 'Veale Gardens'
knows roses that spread past home
she feels the brush of other wings
and the trail that instinct takes them
she sees that colours change at night
with lights she never questioned

in ears held hidden under down,
distress is a foreign tongue
she knows voices that speak only volume
their meaning eclipsed by their noise

despair is crashing glass
a sound that transcends speech
bottles bring a harsher taste than puddle water

Sarah Jane Justice

When I think of Adelaide

When I think of Adelaide I think of my childhood
Christmas holidays and six-hour drives to the big smoke
Toy soldiers and comics to keep me company in the back seat
Winding country roads, the whalebone restaurant at Policeman Point
And then the hills, the lights and Devil's Elbow!

When I think of Adelaide I think of the AMP building
The biggest building we'd ever seen
And we'd always ride it to the top and look out over the city
Dad getting his holiday pay from the bank,
A fistful of redbacks in his pocket
Then off to see the rellies
Swimming pools in Salisbury backyards
With cousins whose names I could never remember
Almond trees at Gawler with the great aunt
And a cast of thousands
Bullens Lion Park at Two Wells
Rundle Street when it ran all the way through

And we'd walk down the sidewalk in awe
Looking at shop fronts we'd never see at home
Coming back with bags and boxes presents and toys
But I still seemed to get second-hand clothes
There were cafeterias and pubs
And right around the corner from my auntie's place
The Green Dragon where dad told me
'Blokes wear dresses in there, mate
So maybe we won't go in tonight'
But we'd be there during the day so I could play the jukebox
And he could have a quiet beer

When I think of Adelaide I think of grand finals
Watching Port Adelaide (the real Port Adelaide) win another flag
And the year I tagged along with dad and his mates
Carnies and ex-sailors at the Semaphore Workers Club
All tattoos and rollie cigarettes
Sneaking me butchers of beer
Walking down the old port with him in awe of those mates
Wharfies and carnies and hardmen who laughed so easily
And showed no fear

When I think of Adelaide I think of long drives from the country
I think of jukeboxes and pubs
And tattooed men who showed no fear
When I think of Adelaide I think of Grand Finals
And sneaking a six-pack into the Flinders Medical Centre
So dad and I could watch one last grand final together
One final beer with a tattooed man
Who still showed no fear
When I think of Adelaide I think of my childhood
Because I want to be young again
And I want him to still be alive

Kami

Adelaide Looming Like a Treasure Chest

I love to cycle, especially in April when the air still holds
summer's scent like a proud train of a gown, the bike path
from Cheltenham to the city trailing quiet streets with houses
to the east & the Outer Harbour line on my right, the ding-ding
of signal crossings melody to a forty-minute dialogue with myself.

At one point the path cuts through a park that is best in April
when the breeze holds its breath only to let it slip slowly out,
cooling shrubbery & skin. There's a stretch where it rises
above the tracks & over South Road, my bike turning mythic
as I cruise above cars & their pollution & the old brick buildings
& the tiny people & I start to pedal faster, like the future is gold.

Heather Taylor Johnson

Day trip

With wonder my guide, I've seen the colours of Mexico…
   The sea
below the cliffs of Croatia… Feathers of exotic birds…
They stain like bright watercolour paint, the paper of my mind.

I've crossed whole oceans and continents… Witnessed the float
of gondolas… How the froth of coffee clings to the lip
in an alleyway café… Red juice of a market barbecue.

But all of this is courtesy of friends' videos… Their happy snaps
and smiles making me cry, 'I went to Elizabeth last week!'
marooned in the mood of circumstance loyal to my everyday…

Town inhabited by my dreams and ideas… People who know
who I am in a railway carriage to Adelaide… My thoughts
inquisitive passengers as I cross a landscape

depicted by graffiti, touching roof-tops and discarded
mattresses… Dry and lifeless backyards replicating the tired
despondency of the needy unemployed… A man

tapping his fingertips on the rail with nodding dark glasses as he
mouths the words of 'fuck the world' rap… The carriage filling
with the beautiful colours and shapes of multi-culturalism…

The wheels click and roll… The view changed to world-class
structures… The Adelaide platform a beckoning sanctuary as I
step away from the train…. Warm sunshine in high glass…

Soft shadows in the leaves of tree-lined streets… The hum
of buses, trams and cars… The uplifting vibe crowding
the footpaths…

Yellow, white, grey and pink chairs under outside tables...
The smells of food and chatter... The reassuring confidence
of men in suits... Confident strut of high heels...

Scooters and bikes... Colour of modern life that takes away
what dogs the mind as I sit here in the summer ambience
of a big country town... A fresh breeze drifting in
from the sea.

Martin R. Johnson

The Argument

There's a miniature rose
in a planter-box in Leigh Street
I want to have picked and given you,
for you to have had, and had had, and held,

though it's still in dirt, in dust, in concrete,
sucking water from the ground
through green décolletage, idly,
crassly, fatuously unaware of how

and why I haven't been arrested
or cautioned by the police, and also

why you're still walking
slightly in front of me
slightly reluctantly
trapping my hand

David Mortimer

Anatomy class

I scuff the leaves along Frome Road:
Doc Marten boots to fit the crowd.
A cold wind blows, the traffic is loud,
my backpack bears a heavy load.
I turn and climb the concrete steps,
push open doors, descend below
to a deeper chill where nothing grows
or moves, to find that all is prepped.
Our sleeping patients bare their arms
to untrained hands and ruthless knives.
Their veins flow with formaldehyde
to hearts that are immune from harm.
I ponder how they spent their lives,
then run to gulp the air outside.

Claire Watson

Room 6, Brookman Ward

for Paige

Once more, I come to read you stories,
as if they could dispense with fear and pain,
as if, somehow, you could be restored to health,

or something that would return you to the life
you had before, where you could be an
eight-year-old again, and do the things

that eight-year-olds do. Today, you are
too sick for this – the lights are off
and the blinds drawn, to keep away the

brightness that hurts, too much, your eyes
and head. You lie, where stories cannot reach,
quiet and still upon your bed, while your dad

speaks to your mum on the phone, telling her
your bone marrow transplant might be deferred;
and though I am intruding upon the scene,

and you barely say a word, the two of you
read your own story to me: the worry in his voice,
the gentle love he has for you, and you for him,

a bond so clear and beautiful, I understand –
the only thing that comforts you today
is this story, this love, and its warm cocoon.

David Ades

Art Gallery and Mitchell Building, c. 1900
(State Library of South Australia, B9192)

For the Moment

Comfort food in the Cathedral Café
After a tiring day at the eye clinic
Around the corner and up the street.
Eye drops make everything blurry,
Hotdog bun crumbs,
Really good coffee.
I finish what mum can't eat.
Tradies come in and out,
My stomach overextends.
I was told one day my sight will fade enough
To take what I've got,
To rob, to stop, to end.
Melancholy is this moment,
Walking back along North Terrace
To catch the bus home.
Mum's always a step ahead of me.
I'm enveloped in tender memories,
Moments of discovery with you.
A rainy date in the Botanic Gardens,
Traipsing through the parklands in the wild wet,
A freak deluge.

I was early for my writer's meeting in
The Cumberland Arms Hotel that night
After we got lost, turned around.
You navigated us safely through.
Familiarity is fairy lights in the trees
On New Year's night,
Walking hand in hand with you
To the G1 bus stop, the place of our first kiss.

This city I've known all my life,
Suddenly, remarkably appears anew.
So it won't cease when my
Sight starts to wane but for the moment
I'm thankful that in the last six months I've been holding,
Stable, mostly unchanged.

Bethany Cody

Starting Over

I fled a marriage empty handed,
leaving family and friends in a country town,
settled close to Adelaide – knowing
I had to work to survive, found a job
working half days at a CBD drycleaners.

The westerlies carried tempting aromas
of syrupy treats cooked in the Pancake Kitchen.
Less lovely, unwanted gifts from pub patrons,
beer or spirits spewed overnight on the doorstep.
In odd moments mending at my sewing machine,
gazed across a quiet pathway at carved stone heads
like gargoyles, high up on the wall opposite,
wondered whose they were; still don't know.
They remain, but that glass frontage morphed
into a louvred hotel loading dock.

Drycleaning shops presented endless chances
for single ladies to meet men bringing in
Hugo Boss and Joseph Uzumcu suits, shirts,
plus stained silk ties impossible to clean.
Didn't tell some that their precious microfibre
was merely rebranded polyester.
When the company franchised that site,
I moved to another off Rundle Mall.

Memories are strong of one festive season,
Myers togged out in Christmas finery,
like an awkward aunty not quite ready to party.

Taped carols played on an endless loop through
a virtual forest of decorations in the Mall
while buskers performed, sometimes between songs,
other times heralding a jarring cacophony.

After that location was also franchised,
the structure altered as if airbrushed.
It's impossible now to even glimpse
a shadow of myself in the picture.

Veronica Cookson

The Map is in My Phone Now: Adelaide By Memory

Into the heart of the beast to gorge on Hungry Jacks and Mc-Donalds on pay day. To linger in the mall near all the shops we couldn't afford to walk inside of. Shame hanging in haloes around our ankles and our wrists. We were just children letting ourselves be kissed.

Remember the first time?
Others jumping the train
Not us
Trying to figure out why
They do it
They did it
Still trying

Smithfield disappears into Elizabeth, into Salisbury, into Parafield Gardens, into Dry Creek, into –

Arriving in that hall
Still takes my breath away
Because,
Because
I remember
Big city, too big
For these hands, these eyes

Hindley Street made of vomit and late-night hell. Made of don't tread alone little girl. And later, made of it's just another foot-path between places. It's just another street full of new faces. The gap between this was then and this is now.

Rundle Mall. I was black jeans and bruises underneath. The city is where the suburbs come to breed. The city is where the dreamers are left to seed. The city is what the country kids thought would set them free.

Time flips the table, scatters mahjong tiles in my hair. I comb echoes in Flinders Street and tickle whispers in Victoria Square. Your open mouths laughing in the sun. My future making a different run. The choice between that was then and who I am now.

It takes time (too much)
To craft a line
Between
Point A and point B
Catching at the pages
Mapping a history,
Ours and mine.

Fifteen disappears into seventeen (baby), into twenty-one (uni attempt one), into twenty-six (the lawns of Government House), into twenty-nine (baby number two), and –

Castle calling on the hill
Turrets to cling to
Words to wring
Wrestle, and
Remember
I keep on
Trying

I hunger for quiet places. Instead, Central Market full of sounds that drown and choke the words. Not made for corners full of bodies and skin and letting the life in. But I do love the noodles there, and the cheese. I slip my hand in his and swallow the sound to now.

Alysha Herrmann

Adornment

Look skywards
through exquisite blooms,
dark branches contrast
against a cloudless sky.

Adelaide's Jacaranda lady
dressed to kill in all her finery,
transforms our streets
into a colour burst.

With the slightest breeze
trumpet shaped flowers,
like purple-blue trinkets
carpet neighbourhoods.

Val Smith

Under the Dome

The rickety-rack of
The Overland is the
Sound of childhood

Life between two cities

Born in Adelaide
Living in Melbourne
Train travel through
The outback – first-class

The arrival platform at
Adelaide Railway Station is
As long as a running track
A greyscale concrete path

The smell of the engine tastes
Like a mouth full of metal braces
Steam dissipates somewhere
Along North Terrace

Three storeys of sandstone
Glows in the rising of the sun
A zephyr gently sweeps its heritage
Since 1856

We meet in the old Waiting Room
The station clock strikes the hour
Under the dome in Marble Hall
A family comes together

Fotoula Reynolds

The Adelaide Taxi Driver's Prayer

after Ian Dury

Our cab fare, which starts in Cavan
Hallett Cove be thy aim
Thy Kingswood come
Thy Willaston
In Hove as it is in Hendon
Give us Largs Bay and Birkenhead
And forgive us our Crafers West
As we forgive those that Crafers against us
And lead us not into Keswick station
But deliver us from Frewville
For thine is the Findon
The Paralowie and the Salisbury
Rostrevor, Rostrevor
Mile End

Mike Hopkins

This Girl is Missing

My brother's accident occurs just over Bordertown. The green car and the white car collide. In the white car a child breaks her leg and is motherless.

In the hospital we wait in the hall and as the walls slide I rest my cheek against the floor, which is cool and solid like so little else. I focus on a sheepskin rug, a bent straw in a cup.

Later I walk out into the night air along a ramp, holding my father's hand. We take great mouthfuls till our lungs hurt. He steers his bulk like a ship and I lean in to his wake.

At first we stay in a motel, but it is too expensive. My father searches for a day, and after this we sleep fitfully in the unfamiliar dark of the People's Palace Hotel.

We visit the museum in the mornings, and in the afternoons we sit by the white bed. I get bored with the water fountain, even the tiny cups.

In the museum I visit the Egyptian Room, while my mother knits in the park. The room is dark with lit tables. Long gold boxes with smooth serious carved faces and black-rimmed eyes.

The People's Palace Hotel is four storeys high. The back stairs are long and precarious. In the Ladies' Room there are two baths, both of them deep and stained, with clawed feet.
We wash in the basin.

All night long there is a shuffling and moaning in the hallway and in the mornings we purchase tickets for breakfast – sausages and toast.

I feel like a queen as I buy opal chips in a street stall and thumb my way through brown paperbacks at ten cents each.

For fifteen days we sit by the white bed. It is necessary, this idleness, like too few seats. A penance for our guilt. My mother says it is rude to ask questions.

Instead of the hospital, one day we take a taxi and search among the tall weeds at the Adelaide cemetery for my grandfather's grave. My mother has a photo and a number.

My parents move rigidly and carefully in this city, on the alert for danger, always careful to brush the dirt of the city off their clothes at night, to wipe the rim of the glass, to keep wide of building sites.

Adelaide is a city of death and accidents and close shaves, a cursed city. My grandfather's pneumonia; my baby sister's camp bed split by a fallen branch. We repeat these stories as we drive across the border in a convoy of concerned relatives.

City of museums and hospitals, city of churches.

In parks and beside the river and in the Square we photograph each other, and wear our best dresses on weekdays, because there are not enough second-best to go around.

In the great hall of the museum there are hundreds of stuffed birds in bits of trees from their natural habitat. In another, the white bones of dinosaurs fill whole rooms right up to the roof. For twenty cents you can hear the sound of bats in a cave.

We take back cartons of freshly squeezed orange juice to our room and drink it from the tiny vegemite glasses on the dressing table that taste of dust.

On Sunday, the sign outside the church says it is the same as ours but inside they drink the communion wine from the little cups one at a time as it is passed around, instead of all together at the end like we do.

This small flaw in the familiarity we seek is somehow even more upsetting than the traffic noise and the shuffling in the hall at the People's Palace.

More upsetting even than the woman with the withered yellow skin who called to us from the steamy depths of one of the baths while we were washing in the basins. 'Pass some soap, love' – her voice dry and cracked. My mother and sister stiffen, and say nothing, but I take the soap to her and get to see the brown patch of hair between her legs and the way it ripples and moves when she reaches across to take the soap from my hand.

In the watery green corridor of the hospital after church, we pass quickly by a grieving family outside a closed door.

Somewhere in the hospital is the little girl from the white car.

At the hotel we watch Homicide on the television, sharing the common room with a group of old men, and my mother cries as George Mallaby is carried out feet first, covered with a white sheet, from a mine accident.

On the news they show another photo of Vicki Barton, and Vicki's mother pleads with the kidnapper to bring her back. Police investigate a lead in Adelaide.

We tell each other how much we hate the city, we are country people. We are just waiting until my brother is well enough to take home.

Every day, the white bed. Every day the same conversation.

We go to church again and this time we drink the wine and replace the cups straight away.

In the museum I put 20c in a slot and hear birds calling to each other in a forest. The stuffed hawk, perpetually swooping over the stuffed mouse...

Until at last the doctor nods, a nurse smiles, and my brother is released. We fly him back across the border, pale now and much thinner.

We talk about the taste of the Adelaide water as the plane hits the runway at Essendon.

And the girl seen in Adelaide is not Vicki Barton after all.

(Have you seen her?)

Beth Spencer

Scot's Church, North Terrace, Adelaide

Familiarity and context
Found in form and structure
A new kingdom (*Terra Australis*)
   the land of the settler
Built on a corner plot
Familiar to the ways of the home country

Ancient etchings
   (well, centuries past)
Inscribed in volumes within
Stained glass telling stories
(Sometimes repeated
   as other church's windows are installed)

Families of the Shepherd
A crofter in retreat in heaven's highlands
His flock scattered:
More than one lost
In the City of Churches

Fraternal connections
Chronicled in the church's records
This marriage officiated within these walls
Links with the past
In this then Presbyterian family
Affirmed in the colony's capital
The groom, born on the Beehive Corner
Many years before
And the bride's Millbrook connection
   (before the reservoir's creation)
A bond between the Scot and English origins
Sealed within a marriage with many children

The bluestone and red brick construction
Limited by the resources of the time
Now a Uniting Church building
Pride of place on the Pulteney Street bend
The castle abutments linking the building's history
With the Highland past
Fitting in readily
Amongst the varsity buildings
On the other side of the Terrace

Alex Robertson

Honey Bee Corner

Honey bee corner
Was where we'd meet
Outside Haighs my favourite place
Staring through the windows
A smile on my face
I'd patiently wait…but
I'd have no control of my feet
They'd take me through Haighs door
The chocolates calling my name
Enticing me again and again
Choc-coated macadamias yes please
Those babies would bring me to my knees
Truffles placed on silver trays
Perfectly lined rows out on display
Cellophane bags fill with choccie delights
Honey bee corner was where we'd meet
Every Friday night
The place where I had no control of my feet

Tracey O'Callaghan

Adelaide, 1970s

I'm watching a man in a grey dustcoat weigh my mother on the great red scales. The needle spins a sigh. Then we mount the speckled marble stairs to Coles Cafeteria, past ladies on public phones, parcels piled at their feet, to a massive room of many voices, chook-house-loud, muffled, shrill. Cups and plates rattle-clanging on stainless steel trays. Chrome chairs scraping. Espresso machines hiss steam at a team of hairnetted staff whose hands are never still. We order pasties, chips and jelly cups.

We 'spend a penny' at John Martin's Ladies' Lounge, then sit plush in a dress circle of lighted mirrors, the air thick with powder and hairspray. I stare into a matrix of mirrored women. If I'm good – really good – and don't tug at my mother's handbag at Moore's closing-down sale where crowds of women fossick amongst the marble pillars for stockings and scarf rings; if I walk all the way to Miller Anderson's, the one-stop-shop for sensibly shod matrons and blue-rinse grannies, then maybe we'll catch the rattly old elevator to heaven, to Cox Foys' rooftop Ferris wheel, which ferries families over the edge and back again.

In Rundle Street – cars fume, buses belch. My hand squeezed tight we cross midstream to buy minimum chips: 15 cents, wrapped in newspaper, an air vent torn in one corner. Groceries in brown paper bags. An STA ticket-seller works the line with his low-slung leather pouch and worn coin sorter. Our bus tickets have messages of wisdom, like *Faith will never die, so long as coloured seed catalogues are printed.*

Down Hindley Street, sleazy young men in nylon body shirts cruise in brown Fords and Sandman panel vans, repeating the same songs on their rock boxes as they loop and leer. There are businessmen in safari suits, wide ties and long socks, joggers in tight bright satin shorts, and platformed women hurrying past in huge sunglasses and boob tubes, careful not to puncture the air with a nipple.

I see Nellie the mechanical elephant smoking at John Martin's Christmas pageant; *Popeye* putt-putting along the Torrens, beside the stick-insect rowers. Upstream, Samorn the zoo elephant dances her rhythms of boredom or takes kids for rides, round and round for a peanut on a post. Naughty boys give her peppered bread. George the orang-utan, sitting with his thoughts.

And back in the suburbs, the postie on a pushbike blows a whistle to warn masses of frenzied dogs. The Tip Top Baker delivers bread in baskets from a slow red van. The bottle-oh calls once a month, tinkles down the driveway, a sackful of brown glass on his back. The milkman rises early to foil the sun and milk-money thieves. Old men ride pushbikes with cartons or kit bags strapped to their carriers. House doors are left unlocked. Asleep on the lawn on summer nights.

A blink and it all turns black and white.

Jude Aquilina

Central Market

It's a summer day.
I am outside heading towards Victoria Square,
It's very busy. Lots of people and traffic around.

I catch the tram from Rundle Mall.
It's hard to get a seat.
I stand and I hold on, so I don't fall over.

The tram is jam-packed full of people.
I want to go to the Central Market and buy some fresh fruit.
Bananas, apples, grapes and pears.

I also get a fresh sandwich.
I find a nice grassy spot to sit and eat it.
The first bite is amazing.

My mouth comes to life.
Hummus, lettuce, carrots, red onion
and you can't forget the sliced bread.
I am glad I got my shopping done
and glad I am not hungry any more.

Tom Cassidy

Hindley Street/Gilbert Place, 2020 (Deb Stewart)

Hindley Street Strut

There's always movement at this station,
Never mind the colts and old regrets,
It starts in the lane near the Pancake Kitchen
And winds around and left and right and up and down
In all five directions at once, milk-shakes and burgers,
Yo-dude hip hop skateboard all excited
Some socialist alliance dalliance, reliance and flog-a-badge…
Uptown downtown round and round lurchy churchy,
There's cops swarming and roosting, ready to flit south –
Car-horn star-worn and old Mo stands, leering at Macca's,
There's a smell of spices no crisis pakora fauna and flora
And Bank Street bars its windows downstairs who cares
And here's the railway underpass, full of cool customers
Trying hard not to run outright out of sight:
Sweet and sour, sleet and scour ciggy wiggy and vego rego,
Some Italian uncles at their coffees,
One has hair another one doesn't, that third one…
Well that's not a wig, that's an exploration,
A planet waiting for the next Cassini fly-by.

Now there's yelling by the Woodshed,
It all sounds like Kay Eff Cee,
And a barrage of bouncers floats up from Red Square,
So let's cross over, drift out past the con brio Rio
As a small samurai shreds Purple Haze
At a cab or two doing kebabs Suburban turban,
A pub crawl natters by in a cloud of Cooperz maaaate.

There's still a bookshop hereabouts for a dive dive dive
(Third World is a distant and sadly missed dream),
Shisha places now, tiny coffees, backgammon and pizza
You know that's NOT smoke, that's hotdogs barking
Past that Christian cinema, so edgy palm trees massage parlour,
There's a 24/7 sun and moon, strip-joint needs a coat of paint
VHS in Korean, Jerusalem with bouncing loungers,
A couple more bars all dogged and ducked
And here's the traffic lights again, some ancient biddy
Looking down from a mural…
Well, there's always movement at this station.

Avalanche

Pancake Kitchen, Gilbert Place

It's odd that the place should still exist
during daylight hours.
Parents lead their children into the sweet warmth:
pancakes and pictures of Alice in Wonderland.

But, were it four a.m. on a Sunday,
it might be us, stumbling down that rabbit warren
reeking liquor in breath and sweat;
laughing about the karaoke bar
and that guy on the corner who said he was God;
gossiping about the girl from school who's getting married
and that other one who died.

Perhaps I am Alice;
lost in a world where mirrors might be doors,
doors might be mouths,
mouths might whisper secrets
and secrets might bite back.
Guided by glimpses of rabbits and cats,
I'm searching for my ace
in a deck that's all jokers…

…or maybe that's just the grog.

Amelia Walker

The Aurora Hotel – History Lost

No regard for salvage
of old glass
or heritage woodwork
or antique iron lace,
all destroyed.

In the middle of the night
early December 1983
the façade of the Aurora Hotel
was demolished
after standing on the corner
of Hindmarsh Square and Pirie Street
since 1859.

Neither petitions presented to parliament
nor Union green bans
nor court injunctions
nor month long pickets
could prevent the obliteration.

The beginning of organised struggles
to save the heritage of Adelaide.

Rob McKinnon

281 Rundle Street

Walking down Rundle, the dawn air brims
with coffee, stale beer and freshly washed bitumen.

I step through the veil between this world and memory
and the street is heady with cabbage, chaff

and the jostling wafts of exhaust and compost.
From The Stag, past Lemongrass to Eros Kafé,

beneath the stomp of my stride, I can hear
the grumble of Bedford flatbeds, men's laughter

and the clang of grocers' trollies echoing under
that vast iron roof while the morning dark hovers

at the Market's edges. On this stretch of footpath,
my hand always feels naked. It should be held.

A callused palm means safety. But history is vapour.
My aunt insists that Silbert, Sharp & Bishop,

where Grandpa worked for forty years, was on the right
of Frank's Lane. But I remember tripping across

that great steel plate in my shiny red shoes,
his workmates chuckling when the needle

of the huge commercial scale barely flinched.
I was sure it was the left. I'm wrong.

It's La Taberna now. Only yesterday it was Cocolat.
And just a blink before that, I dug beneath it all

as an archaeologist, wincing every time
my boss said *colonial slum*. She sent me to dig

the greasy black mire of the tannery where,
in my filthy overalls, I unearthed a toy horse,

then, hours later, its rider. Reuniting those tiny friends
thrilled the child in me, that same excited girl whose hand

Grandpa would hold tight through the Parkland's
storybook dark as he led me to the bright clamour

of the East End Market, where strange languages
huffed in tiny clouds and men, cabled and scratchy

in hand-knitted wool, would pinch my cheeks rosier
than a red delicious. *Bella bambina! Ómorfo koritsáki!*

My pinafore pockets bulged with their gifts. Apples.
Peaches. As the world beyond the trucks and traders

found its daytime shape and the pigeons snuggling
on the great roof joists flapped themselves awake,

Grandpa would lead me down Rundle Street, dawn light
flushing gutters clotted with cabbage and carrot top.

In the fogged warmth of Ruby's Café, the adventure
closed with toasted sandwiches and lace-trimmed socks

swinging on the chrome stool while we waited for the beep
of Grandma's Cortina. Tucked beneath her soft arm

I'd be asleep before the last grand gum of the Parklands
ghosted my window. Now, my worn boots stride past Gorman,

Bauhaus and M.J. Bale, where the perfume of wealth masks
the whiff of tanning pit. At Frome, I wait at the lights.

By the Austral, memory's breath of cabbage dissolves, but not
that ache to once more feel his hardened hand hold mine.

Rachael Mead

Rundle Street

Two men
sipping coffee
at midnight

one smokes fiercely
looks always in front
never behind

points at a window
describing his escape

counts on his fingers twice
the years of exile

hacks at his arm, his leg
to show how lucky he is

pulls at his false teeth
that is all he has to show
after all the beatings

maps his journey
on the tabletop

dabs at his eyes
as he tells how
he returned too late
to save his mother

points to heaven
to give thanks
for his good fortune.

Julia Wakefield

Rundle Mall

Three boys lurking
in kitchen appliances
two in their early teens
one still a child
two mousy-haired
one redhead
fingering packaging
measuring lengths
the young one on guard
elbows the redhead
they scatter silently
the shop assistant
ambles down the aisle
rearranges the knives
glances casually around
the empty shop.

Julia Wakefield

Him

...an isolated hiccup in reality's shining surface
runs like ripples o'er the crystalline darkness of the truth...

It is Him.

Him the prophet lunatic, clad
in leotard
gumboots
and not much else...

He parts the waters
merely with His presence
as static shockwave silence
rips
along the shallow depths of Rundle Mall.

Prickling whispers proclaim horror
to mask the horror
of not being horrified
but strangely somehow envious

that He can simply walk
desiring not pity or honour
He can simply walk
away...

And after He is gone
remain
for the crowd still speak of Him
still analyse His plight.

Some call Him mad
or the only one sane
others say madness is universal
but few possess strength to confess it.

And I heard from a friend
          of a friend
          of a friend
          of a friend…

really, he just does it for a bit of a laugh.

Amelia Walker

Full circle

An icon
or monstrosity, depends
on what you want to see. I rubbed its
shimmer as a girl; the silver wonder was
unfurled the very year that I was born, to
bright applause and bawdy scorn. The 'Mall's
Balls' claimed the naked space, and soon became
a meeting place that knocked the Beehive down
a peg. Its glossy mirrors slimmed your legs and
swelled your middle. My whole world
reflected back in coloured
swirls. My mother
gripped
my eager hand, and
led me through a foreign land
of Balfour's cakes and perfumed haze,
piano men in swish DJ's. My father worked in
Grenfell Street, amongst the suits and hurrying
feet. I spied my boyfriend in the crowd, below a
sphere of shining clouds. He led me far from my
birthplace, and other landscapes I embraced.
Although three states I since have
roamed, magnetic steel
compels me
home.

Claire Watson

Frog Cakes

after Balfours Tea Rooms in Rundle Street (1856–2004)

Submerged in the sweet shallow
crowded pond of shopfront display.
Cold in green-iced skin;
their slightly parted cake lips
croak on a string of silent years.
And they are an icon for each –
connecting fairy tales with Christmas
Mother with Myers.
And finally lunch at Balfours
where they became for us, the small
luxury she could afford – cramming
our mouths with their confection; and
always looking better
than they tasted!

Jeff Guess

On the Torrens

See how the artist has caught
that tamarisk on canvas,
articulating the space
between the cascading pink fronds
at the water's edge
and the waters murky beneath,
how he has sent the bridge soaring,
all struts and lines and angles,
throwing weight to the winds,
how he's pictured the quiet pleasure boat,
traced people on the pathway
and tried to capture that little girl.
But she has managed
to rearrange the scene;
drawn into the foreground
with a shimmer of movement
she has dispensed with symmetry
and form. Her body a brushstroke,
her dress a drift of colour,
she had set in motion
the seagulls at her feet

Elaine Barker

The bird of prey, the blackbird, the magpie

I miss you.

I see
the sandy brown bird of prey,
the blackbird,
the magpie
with wings outstretched
flying under white clouds
on a sea blue sky
filling the back brick wall
of townhouses
on Morphett Street.

I miss you.

I remember the empty space
beside this brick wall where
I could see a clear view of you
from the bus window
on my way to the city.
the bird of prey,
the blackbird,
the magpie.
What is your story?
What is your story?

I miss you.

I remember construction workers.
A tower of concrete, steel and glass
replace the empty space
trapping you in darkness.
the bird of prey,
the blackbird,
the magpie.

I miss you.

I feel a sense of loss and sadness.
I won't see you again.
I have no photos of you.
Just a memory. My memory of you.

I will miss you.
the bird of prey,
the blackbird,
the magpie.

Stella Damarjati

The Walk On By Blues

The CBD and State Library

Vistas of golden sands
on the travel centre billboard,
promise of golden lands
on the travel centre billboard,
a man asleep on the concrete
out of the rain and autumn chill.

His body bunched up tight
under a stained and dusty jacket,
fraying shoes no longer white
and a stained and dusty jacket,
belongings stashed away
inside a lumpy denim sack.

Families and couples
strolling past him on a night out,
gastronomes and clubbers
rolling past him on a night out,
they look beyond or frown upon
this unexpected blight.

Walk on by, he shouldn't be here.
Walk on by, he might be mad.
Walk on by,
we're in a hurry
and we're paying all our taxes
and there's nothing we can do
but walk on by.

A photographic show
in a corner of the library,
muffled voices from below
in the foyer of the library,
a man asleep beneath a picture
of a timeless sea and sky.

Looking quite at home
in repose on the carpet,
shoes off and neatly ranged,
in their place, on the carpet,
his coat draped on a chair,
and his phone plugged in to charge.

Security comes down,
looks away and leaves him,
the guard just glances round,
goes on his way and leaves him,
ensures no one disturbs him
but pretends he doesn't see.

Walk on by – you look OK here.
Walk on by – it's rather sad.
Walk on by –
you're dry and warm there
and we close up in an hour
but for now you'll have some peace.

I'll walk on by.

Sharon Foulkes

Near the Topham Mall Car Park

I feel for the homeless man
sleeping on a bench in Topham Mall.
Theatregoers head back to their cars.
He is wallpaper
unseen
ignored by passers-by.
But they see,
they know.
They do not stop,
do not help.
Nor do they know his story.
It may be wild
or may be sad
Or just maybe
it might be theirs.

* Collaborative poem written by participants in Deb Stewart's workshops for the Adelaide City Library/Spoken Word SA Poet-in-Residence program.

South bank of the Torrens showing huts occupied by
homeless men during the 1930 depression
(State Library of South Australia, B5800)

Resilience

For years now I have seen him walking along South Terrace, up Hutt Street then threading his way down Halifax or Angas Streets, his footsteps haunting the city pavements. Always the same pace, one foot then the next, measured steps, even strides. Head bent towards the ground, he does not look to the left or right. He always has an air of purpose about him as he takes his daily constitutional. He has come from the beautiful south park-lands, the place he calls home. He appears to favour this south-eastern corner of the city for his walking and is 'known' by many.

> beneath a shady tree
> he sleeps, the song of birds
> in his ears

He is always dressed the same. A long dark coat, summer and winter. His skin is walnut brown and his hair hangs in long dreadlocks down his back. No shoes. Never any shoes. I marvel at how his feet must have hardened over time. How resilient he appears to be. He is not a young man but possibly chooses to remain barefoot.

His steps take him past Cibo, packed with al fresco coffee drinkers chatting away about their office politics, or what to wear to the pub tonight, or how some friends have just bought a new car. I wonder if they spare him a thought as they sip their latte or long black?

> they talk
> their superficial talk
> pretend they have not seen him pass

Do they avert their faces with disdain at the matted hair that darkens the shoulders of his coat? Are they concerned about where he eats and sleeps? If he goes to the Hutt Street refuge and tucks into one good meal a day? At the centre everybody is respected and encouraged, no matter who they are or how they are dressed.

Often I have seen him over near Victoria Square amongst the office workers. They move to avoid him, conscious of his feet, bare and dirty, toes stiff with winter cold.

> where others push trolleys
> their lives in plastic striped bags
> he walks empty-handed

I often think about how his story might have evolved, how he became homeless and if he has dreams other than surviving each day from hunger and the weather.

> have his dreams been
> long forgotten
> dissolved in winter rain

Jill Gower

The Adelaide City Baths – post-mortem

Torn down.
Ripped up.
Pulled apart.
All directions were implicated
in my destruction.
So that now
nothing remains but space –
a 'Plaza', a car park.
Really? Is that the best you could do?
It's such a belly flop, an insult
to the memories I held,
the swimming champions I fostered,
the perfect arcs that divers followed.

Oh, yes. I know…
The changing city demographics,
suburban developments,
and, doubtless, my modernist façade
looked unbecoming in 1969.
But replacing all I was
with emptiness?

I was condemned.
But so are you.

Bruce Greenhalgh

CBD Reality

A constant two-way
flow of people.
Rundle Street, Adelaide.
Where are they going?
Where have they been?
Street people
moving somewhere
through the CBD
reality frame.

The old musician
strums his guitar,
amplified softly, battling
against the Subway music
box, and news that the
big game at the stadium begins
in thirty minutes!

Still they come with that pace
that determines they are not beach
walkers drifting, but committed
pram pushers, bag carriers.
Commuters on the
treadmill of CBD travellers
between nowhere and a
somewhere
known only to them.

A classic orange Ford
Mustang screams towards
the traffic lights.

Vroom! Vroom!

'The Sound of Silence'
via Disturbed, echoes
from the Subway music box.

Nothing
stops the reality of the endless flow.

Martin Christmas

Grenfell Street

A pace to the left but adrift,
back to a granite façade
cold, slick as the commerce within
his face crumpled as a pie bag
he fights voices flat as slate
that mutter behind his eyes,
prise away sanity's nails and hooks;
oblivious to footpath people a nod away,
who scurry through mazes of make and break;
dare not discard masks
to glimpse the barbed wire of tomorrow –
today's entanglements always enough
to forgo steps closer to him –
let alone themselves.

David Cookson

Devil's Elbow

1.

It curves like a ribbon round the neck of the hill
then slides round its sides to the rib of the road.

I can get there with my eyes closed.

Wild and free – it is deadly.
In the fractured hour I turn into its tight grip.

Sometimes there is a poem there, or sex scene.
Words. Not real. Just written.

You prefer real?
Often, it is the only way.

2.

We speed on a HWY with the windows down.
'Romanian Rhapsody' is on the radio and
sunrays are playing hit and miss
across the windscreen.
You place your arm around my seat and
we turn to each other knowingly.
Departing is a daily rehearsal.

At night, we drive back
to tomorrow.
Sitting statuesque, headlights
defeated by the distance of roads
and slightly further from you
I am dream driving.

My bat black hair is escaping
through the window.
All hair is dead.
This casualty is nobody's fault.

3.

Stop saying it is nobody's fault.
Words sound like staged collisions.

No broken bones, but the heart is not a bone.
If dislocated, it will be a long recovery.

You must be versatile.
Risk a turn. Drive back.

To days spent reconstructing
your mind, setting it in the right direction.

See if there is anything
in the dead end street.

A resting point.
For now.

I watch you walk away –
not even a scratch.

You are welcome.

4.

There is history.
The streets know.

Once I pulled over.
Watched a hitchhiker
under the light.

From A to B
then back to me
was as far as I got.

5.

Steer yourself away from my line.
I am writing my way back.

All the vehicles are suddenly scrap paper.
I search them forensically.

At the intersection on South Terrace
I lean on the wheel and watch

the statue of a woman
a bling of promise in the sun

even if coming back
defeats the purpose of going forward.

This morning, there was a pillow on the grass.
Someone woke up and left.

6.

I trace the passenger seat and remember
my daughter measuring
how long until her feet reached the floor.

Driving from school.
The years.
The life lessons.

Jelena Dinic

Whitmore Square

This night.
On my seat.
In the bus.
I gaze out to Whitmore Square.
Colourful light bulbs
hang from electrical wires
from light pole to light pole.
Burning bright.
Red, orange, yellow, green.
Lighting the path.
Lighting the path.
A sight of wonder
in my mind.
Of magic in summer.
Of magic in summer.

Stella Damarjati

Parklands

A huddle of shadows
under the ghost gum
three men
two women sit
in the present
watching
the past
they are still here when
the traffic rushes home
they have been here since
the dawn of time

Julia Wakefield

The Aboriginal Flag in Victoria Square

Aboriginal people
on the red earth
under the life-giving yellow sun.

Harold Thomas's design
of identity and expression,
a symbol of unity and resistance
for a people's collective struggle
flying in Victoria Square
since 12 July 1971.

Rob McKinnon

'Soldiers Lot'

Australian Imperial Forces (AIF) Cemetery, West Terrace Cemetery

Alongside the ten-metre-high
Angaston marble
Cross of Sacrifice
the Australian flag flutters,
towering over 4167 graves
of returned service men and women
from the Great War.

Surrounded by sculptured hedges
including a seedling
related to the Lone Pine in Gallipoli
with neatly cut lawn,
the long rows of white headstones
shine in the sun,
some names and details now faded.

Did they go to fight for King and country
or for the fear of being called a coward
or just for the adventure?

Physical scars were obvious
but the haunting horrors of war
were rarely shared.

Rob McKinnon

Sandalwood

Padipadinyilla Park, North Adelaide

Midsummer has blistered the hills,
scorched the plains, has for a while
flaked colour from the park.
Even the dust smells pale,
grasses grow taut and white.
Late in the day three women venture out,
their saris of iridescent crimson,
magenta, scarlet and gold.
So that their warmth seems greater
than the surrounding heat –
fecund and all-embracing.
A sudden breeze stirs their silks
to rise and fall, to stream away
shimmering, to melt into light.
The cloth ripples as it flows, whipped up
and lapping over leaves and bark
and those very small gumnuts
clustered along the path.
The women's shadows are lengthening
as they pass. I am breathing in
their laughter, a jingle of bangles,
the perfume they've put on.

Elaine Barker

Alchemy

Oh, Adelaide.
How predictable you are.
Your today is like your yesterday
and last year's March the ninth.

But I'm glad
your railway station ramp
still swallows commuters whole.

Glad, too,
that your statue
of that soldier on his horse
(rearing, as if alarmed by a right turning tram)
remains on the corner.

I'm amused that
your town planning Rubik's cube,
Victoria Square,
still defies all attempts
to breathe life into its centrality.

I'm waking up thinking
I need more sleep
and thankful that
you expect so little from me.

Please know
the feeling's mutual.

Bruce Greenhalgh

Adelaide Railway Station

I'm lumbering up Adelaide railway station's ramp
cringing with each lunge movement
cursing my PT
thinking 'nothing's ever easy';
My legs hurt
I am determined to reach the top.
Breathe
breathe
push on regardless.
A welcome challenge: the ramp
for the hearty and the fit
C'mon.
Don't give up.
Nearly there.
It's clear
I need another sesh with the PT!

* Collaborative poem written by participants in Deb Stewart's workshops for the Adelaide City Library/Spoken Word SA Poet-in-Residence program.

City Baths, 21 May 1941
(State Library of South Australia, B10492)

North Terrace

Come, live this mile with me.

Leave your childhood here with its creatures and flowers, the
paths you sprinted, all the trees you climbed.

Teach yourself, research, learn, aspire, work to be more than
you think you can be.

Admire paintings, trace pasts, run your fingers through
fountains, sit and read a while.

Stop to reflect, head bowed and quiet, salute those before
you, then play.

Protest on steps, for the climate, fair pay, give power to those
feelings it stirs up inside you.

Day trip by train to broaden your blue and return to risk
something more.

Stroll round conventions, absorb seminars, talks, contemplate
life and all you have done.

Now time to rest, feel this falling away, and dream of weather
bursting words at your feet.

J V Birch

Beatlemania

from the verse novel *An Adelaide Boy*

I've never seen anything like the crowd
that filled the city on that Friday in '64
to greet the Beatles at the Town Hall.
Surely every person in Adelaide was there
lining the streets on that sunny winter day
I wasn't a huge fan then but Frank, my brother, was
and so I tagged along for the walk
to King William Street, moving with the human tide
grateful to be living on the edge of town
with no need to catch a bus or try to find a park.
For me it was an excuse to wag school
maybe brush with fame or meet some girls.
We could hear the screaming a mile away
it was manic for sure, hard to believe
that four guys from the UK could incite such a roar
I was a little peeved that Ringo couldn't come
at the time he was the one I admired the most
as I fancied myself a drummer, despite not even having a kit.
Later, of course, I grew to appreciate the Beatles more
and George was the one who stirred my awe.

There was no hope of talking to girls that day
their sights were firmly fixed on the coming cavalcade
then to the Town Hall balcony and those guys in suits
who could have been anyone from a distance
just ordinary men with extraordinary fame.

I wasn't a huge fan but that day I became a part
of the writhing, screaming, hysterical sea of Adelaideans
jostling for a glimpse of their fave band
even returned the next afternoon,
as the shops on Rundle Street were closing,
to stand on the steps of Parliament House
hoping that the Fab Four were indeed
in the hotel across the road
that I might catch sight of them again
to be forever connected with this pinnacle
of Adelaide's musical history.

Deb Stewart

State Library Mortlock Wing

A mustiness of books seeps from cloth covers,
wrought iron mezzanines tumble in tapestries
from grimy skylights and coffered ceilings,
ice-blue halogens drench leathered red-gum benches,
students spill from alcoves.

> *The Adelaide Circulating Library*
> *will strictly enforce a fine*
> *of twopence a day for overdue books*
> *Subs are seven shillings per quarter*

Mysteries whisper like mice
through endpapers on the west wall racks,
Adventures stride with heavy-bound tread down the aisle,
blood-red boards throb with Romance in dark corners,
regiments of War Stories encircle the stair

> *Any subscriber lending this book*
> *to any non-subscriber not a member*
> *of the subscriber's household will*
> *render himself liable to expulsion*

The Mortlock Wing is imprinted with autumn
as books bear the librarian's enduring stamp,
offering refuge from the steel and glass
foraging area of monitors and data bases,
a watering hole in a sweating swirling city.

Roger Higgins

10.31

Sudden surge through gates.
Older, younger, carry bags,
satchels, cases, kids, babies
in strollers. Turnstile
click of cards.
Tread of cycles.
Human wave.
Footfall.
Chatter.

10.32
A sort of stillness descends
to begin again
when the next train
comes into Adelaide
Railway Station.

Sign reads,
Gawler. Departs in 1 minute.

Out of the blue next to me
a Metro transport surveyor.
Question one, 'How do you find
public transport?'
I answer, 'I don't use it much.'
She exits.

Three burly police officers
materialise, observe me
scribbling in a black notebook
suspiciously.

I stop writing poetry
returning to the real world.

Martin Christmas

After Adelaide Writers' Week

West Stage

Half open, the dark green metal gates allow me to enter
no volunteer in a pale green shirt to greet me
no walk through an archway of sticks today
no blue sails above, for the sun to blast through gaps
instead of chairs and assorted audience
parallel patterns of pale brown, curved lines
left behind by the scuff of feet
greener where the chairs were
the only voices now are distant ones

East Stage

Foot traffic has taken its toll
a large patch of almost mud
sprinkled with bright yellow leaves
occasional orange and red
no microphones
the brown grass signals
where the stage was
favoured listening spots
on the slope behind
are marked out
in various shades of brownish green
people stroll on the path above
no children roll down today

The Book Tent

For a week this rectangle of grass
kept closer company
with books than with the sun
I sit where the entrance was
near the signing table spot
I notice a slight crackle
rain on dry leaves
a single raindrop
spots my jacket
one curled brown leaf
floats to the ground
traffic noise
in patches
is ocean
a plover bobs along

Memories

Debates begun
questions posed
laughter shared
woven through the garden
settled
in the bricks
and plaques
in the leaves
and sharp shadows
the recent bloom of a tiger lily
Ola Cohn's statue of a woman

Kylie Dinning

Living Collections

WOMADelaide, Botanic Park

Under friendlier trees and a fiercer sun,
Sam Lee resurrects these fragments of melodies,
memories mined from transplanted wanderers.
Wisps of song-stories uncorked from their guardians
seem to meander up from the past
and hang.

Some ancient rhythm rules the harp,
untappable.
The fiddle sighs and teases,
unpredictable.
Surely momentarily they'll break into a jig –
under friendlier trees and a fiercer sun?

But in the wistful dappled silence of a pause,
primordial beats and cheers pulse the breeze,
as Kutcha's rockin' on a distant stage somewhere –
another grounded nomad gets back up again.

But unsubdued, Sam's tunes go lilting still,
telling of twilight and love unrequited,
under friendlier trees and a fiercer sun.

Sharon Foulkes

Botanic Gardens in Limelight

The Italian garden:
a courtyard in a secluded spot,
fountains and ponds.
Sculptures rest elegantly
on pedestals, amid leafy alcoves.
Purple and gold, rich Roman hues
abound in this quiet place.

Gardens in their prime,
flowers bloom, wisteria in bowers,
winding pathways,
a trail of nature in abundance.

Roses in a whirl circle the lawns.
Red, mauve, yellow, white, arches of colour.
Each one nurtured, its petals ablaze,
fragrant and aromatic.

The crystal shape of the Palm House
like a jewel newly restored,
is a sparkling backdrop.

I love walking in the garden,
beside lakes with ducks,
birds and swans, age old trees and palms.

The myriad species,
hues, shapes, and sizes.
A masterful scene.
Most of all,
there is peace and serenity.

Airlie Kirkham

Palm House

I met you there one day

In the glass Palm House in the garden

Sunbeams scattered and filtered your face
The lines of people showed you the way
Up the stone steps, in through the doors
I wondered if that's what this glasshouse was made for

So I could meet you

I met you there one day

When spring had just begun, and jasmine scented the breeze
The blue in your eyes brought me to my knees
We made whimsical memories in a glass house shipped from
    Bremen
And if I could reverse time, I'd do it all again

So I could meet you

I met you there one day

When our hearts were still so pure and young
And our remarkable love story had just begun
We mused over magic, stars and the moon
And when we parted ways you said we'd meet again soon

I met you there one day

In the glass Palm House in the garden

Lauren Bronwyn Wagner

Moon lantern

OzAsia Festival

Take
me down
to the Torrens
where the
lanterns burn
tonight
where colours
dance on water
threaded with
moonlight

walk me
past the crowds
into Elder Park
over grass
cool and green
hold my hand
and lead me
through the parade
into a dream

take me down
to the river
with the lanterns
aglow tonight
release the dragon
into my mind
rippling reflections
erupt into fiery flight.

Shaine Melrose

The big city lights

Big city skyscrapers
Back in 1986 our arrival
Double lanes on Franklin street
Country girl meets city life
It took a while for me to find my feet
Trains buses public transport I'd never seen that
Rundle Mall with its big balls
Botanical gardens right in the middle
Breath taking picturesque and serene
Parts of the city were like a dream
The city of churches
Heritage buildings galore
Cultures so diverse different nationalities
Filling the streets
These were the people I was eager to meet
Music blasting from discotheques
To us it was the city that didn't sleep
Slow walks through the mall
High heels in our hands bare feet
6 a.m. heading home
Bus money all we had left
After dancing our feet off
At all those discotheques

Charles Sturt Richmond
The mansion Grenfell tavern
Down all those stairs we went
Adelaide the city it was a delight
Partying every Saturday night
Popeye cruises on the Torrens
Paddleboats I fell in
A lingering kiss in the rotunda
At Elder Park in the early hours
Of the morning
While it was still dark

A pie floater outside the train station
The best in the nation
They warned me about Hindley Street
But I wasn't told about the people
Sleeping on park benches that I'd meet
I stood and stared
Not out of disrespect
I was in shock
Horrified at the neglect
I refused to believe us humans
Allowed it to get like this
Country girl as green as could be
What I saw
Truly affected me

Tracey O'Callaghan

Popeye

Motor launches on the River Torrens

As a child I believed the captain
at the boat's wheel: peaked cap;
short-stemmed pipe against the wind;
had the best job in the world.

On those cold dark mornings –
from wooden landing to the zoo;
hidden, overgrown banks opened like
secret detail from old picture books.

I had the story of the drowned boy –
his legs tangled helplessly in weed
as a cautionary tale from my grandmother:
the opaque river still gave little away.

Strange and decay: slicing a quicksilver
surface – sailing into perfectly preserved
branches of bare winter willows;
last leaves clotting with the mud.

An arrow of mallard ducks,
a grey slippery flash of water rat,
the boat stopping somewhere
before a bridge where the river went on.

One thing I knew for certain –
if I were captain
one morning I wouldn't stop but sail
beyond the bridge as far as I could get.

That fantastic journey as a child,
that exists in one simple move forward –
time complicated with strong currents and
the weight of obstacles against the boat.

Jeff Guess

The Gallerie

'You'll like our style'

1. Prologue

A long-defunct shopping centre
may seem a strange place
to paeanise but once upon a …
its bustle of gleaming tiles, white
marble & shiny brass handrails
made it the coolest place in my world
(Australia's first Wendys, Orange Julius
with its overtacky plastic oranges
& crazy chicken-salt chips, Eliza's,
a vego place whose name I forget
that made a yummy brown rice
& vegie pie, Clip Joint on the mezzanine,
Carla Zampatti's, florist, café,
deli sort of store, Greek takeaway
& so many forgotten more)
but sometimes things grease
themselves so deep into memory
more profound reminiscences
have trouble sticking

2. Oscar's Coffee shop

Where a cocky country kid
discovered Vienna coffee
in a tall glass extravagance
& where we went on our
first date before we knew
it was one – Oscars
tucked away, up the stairs,
round the corner, over
looking Gawler Place
seemed so cosmopolitan
to that insecure young man
who spent endless hours
there lost in your lioness laugh

3. Food Court

straight down from North
Terrace a glorious subterranean
food palace full of amazing taste
promises though nothing beat the first
takeaway on the left – Yuan House:
Home of Authentic Mongolian Food
uncertain of this claim's veracity
but know
whenever I had their Mongolian
meatballs after a dull Adelaide
Uni lecture I felt the breeze
of the Mongolian steppes disturb
my already disturbing mullet

4. Epilogue

also know Yuan House
was where I spent
too much time sitting
where we used to sit
trying to bring it all back
cos while I'm there
the ghosts don't dare
push me too far…

Gareth Roi Jones

The Spheres by Bert Flugelman (aka 'Malls Balls'),
Rundle Mall, 2020 (Deb Stewart)

Hamlet 2018

Being or, in the Dress Circle, examining
not to be, through more than three hours,
with a break to buy lollipops, 'a sung play'
my wife remarked, as we raced for the late train
with the sound of the Angels pumping across the water
from Adelaide Oval, despite all of Dean's opera, Armfield's
sets and Shakespeare's words, finding ourselves singing
to the sky and street trees on the way home
'Am I ever gonna see your face again?'

David Mortimer

65 King William Street

A home to many, a haven
For those who craved
A place to rest for a couple
Of years, then move on.

Or one where talents
In thinking, and drinking
Merged, at end of week,
Knock off, head for Tavern,

Get a drink, sit down, chat.
Get another, stay awhile,
Going over week's doings,
Then catch a bus home…

The ATO, clerks with eyes
On power, clerical assistants
With eyes on the weekend
Powerless ones, unless

They stuck there long enough,
Learnt the ropes, moving
Through the ranks, ever upward
Or just stayed, powerless…

Fond memories, of eighteen floors
Of friendship, drama, but also
Boredom too, filing, delivering,
Down stairs or up them, constant.

It's changed now, the Tax Office,
Split up, moved, some of us
Gone, retired, but get together
Once a year, to relive it all…

Glory days, or not, the ATO
still lives large in memories
Of those of us who gave it
Our best, or looked like we did!

Carrying a folder, or paper
And pen at least, stood in
For 'working', hiding any
Shirking, as things got done

Or didn't, and as long reports
Were reported to government
Showing the actions were
Undertaken, results attained

Or reasons why, given, if not.
Five days a week, the lifts going
Up and down, up and down,
Few seeing view from the roof…

Carolyn Cordon

City Street Sweeper

He does Grenfell Street and Rundle Mall
and could find any doorway, blind but
he has to point for the tourists – only
his English for 'excuse me' is perfect.

Dealing with its dirt he is
daily exposed to its weaknesses:
secrets he scrubs from street corners;
dry leaves that rattle after bones.

He limps behind his broom
from an old early Sunday morning
stab wound: a splintered blade
the legacy of lameness in his thigh.

Been bashed once too, and knows
the bad side; the drink and drugs;
kids that break all of the little laws;
the crunch of needles in soft dark.

But this morning it is spring again:
a road barrow sways heavy with fruit;
and the girls are all dressed this year
in colours of the sky and clouds.

And he is an old man who came in '52
from southern Greece to make a life:
his kids have grown up and away;
while his wife went back to Salonika.

Sometimes he thinks now the city is all
that he has left, and he will say
he loves her like a woman;
but has also got to like her as well.

Jeff Guess

Living under water during drought

each tramcar platform in King William Street
is besieged by schoolkids
tropical fish in school colours
that swim and swarm
below the waveform dip and rise
of wires and cables that distort the sky

the brightly painted trams
are nudibranchs that creep and pause
creep and pause from reef to reef
until at Glenelg their tentacles sense
seagrasses and leafy dragons
so they pause and creep away

backlit clouds smudge the horizon
we are in a hot haze between sea and sky
between wet and dry
we struggle for breath with tight lips
while in flared nostrils
the smell of rain would be heaven sent

Roger Higgins

Adelaide

after Kevin Hart

I travelled to a city made of sand,
Cried till Nhill, but by Murray Bridge, dry-eyed.
Glared at my lost mum, said, *I smoke this brand.*
Gleeful, Mum simply mocked, *Well, so do I.*

Begged Dad to turn back until Kaniva.
Gully wind whispers, it's the trees that rant.
Gleeful, Mum simply mocked, *Well, so do I.*
Dreams get carried away here by bull ants.

Gully wind whispers, it's the gums that rant.
School lunch cut by Ex-SAS stepdad.
My worries too, carried off by bull ants,
While Marley nights drank all the Mum we had.

Stepdad was cutting fritz when doorbell rang,
Aunty rocked into town in snakeskin pants.
We half-sisters laughed all night as Mum sang,
By morning Aunt had slammed her caravan.

Aunt shrewdly squeezed into red leather pants,
Family day on the Torrens, paddleboats;
Through a bar window she once threw a man,
Now in revenge, spruced up for casino.

Bridging worlds – on the Torrens, boats to let,
Then to ancient flamingos at the zoo.
Mum tight-lipped; Aunt whisked me off for roulette,
Night's end, flew through saloon doors to spew.

Ancient and blind, *Stay* – flamingos rail,
As Mum turned her hourglass of quicksand.
Stacking her winnings, Aunt said, *Stick to tails*.
Cried till Wail, by Nhill lost sight of myself.

Jen Allen

Cold Front

The wind breaches a long blue calm, shoulders
hard into morning, sweeps inland drawing
gusty breaths. An unleashed sea piledrives waves

upon the coast. Clouds gather, violet dark,
coalesce, slate seal a seamless sky. Stripped
of light, city streets brood colourless,

traffic congeals space in radial lines
spun from intersections, pedestrians
shelter thoughts behind dull pavements.

A moment arrives, wedged between wind and clouds,
when there is a lull, the hush between breaths.
Distances are string-pulled tight around the

arch of the sky. A yellow greening belt
of parklands and gardens encircles
the city with fingers of silence, sheds

russet stained leaves in slow spirals. Swallows
dart and swoop low, dark blue-tinged arrow streaks.
A grove of trees brushstroked Van Gogh gold raises

cupped hands skyward, hairline fissures cobweb the
ground opening the earth's gills, and with a diving
slice through air of downward wings, the rain comes.

David Ades

Rain on Rundle

In old Rundle Street,
pedestrians squeeze and bump
bustling bodies
under canopies,
seeking shelter from the rain.

It still rains in Rundle Mall
buskers hide
under inadequate shelters
and covet corporate umbrellas.

In summer the sun is avoided,
pedestrians seek shade.

* Collaborative poem written by participants in Deb Stewart's
workshops for the Adelaide City Library/Spoken Word SA
Poet-in-Residence program.

Balls

After the sculpture by Bert Flugelman, Rundle Mall (1977)

An unlikely conjunction
of two silver spheres
that interprets the shops
and passing parade –
pulling faces;
and each leg that passes.

A meeting place for lovers
who waiting
affect the gentle ambient
curving round. Made for hands.
Cleavage and weight.
A cold icon of desire.

Two bulging fish-eyes
in a strange sea of reflection,
that wraps this street:
twin hemispheres of abstract
expression. Mad lidless lenses
that show just what they see!

Jeff Guess

in her words

chilled city
street scape
early mid-morning
café searching
hunger suppressant
coffee fix

homelessness
settles unreasonably
and palpable disadvantage
aggravates sidewalk sojourn
but unthinkable
if invisibility scores

Geoff Aitken

The Turban

I thought of you again today and the way,
as an older man, you sat straight and tall and bearded,
alone on a wooden bench in the Mall.

You were well-dressed but stood out for
the twisted length of cotton, meticulously folded,
that formed the covering for your head.

As you watched the passers-by did you observe
a drabness that made you yearn for your homeland
and the crescendo of colours there?

You were part of our urban life
yet seemingly apart, as if piecing things together
and waiting for wisdom to come.

And I could have bent and spoken to you
but it would have seemed an impertinence,
an intrusion. It was unnecessary.

Now years later I am writing in celebration
to say you're not forgotten. I took delight
in your composure. And your bright purple turban.

Elaine Barker

No Through Road

The stench of diesel fuel
assails the nostrils.
Bus after bus idles,
picking up
the standing trade.

CBD Adelaide.

T-shirt scribbles
by the score.
Go Round – wobbly breasts.
Oakley – tall and skinny guy.
88 – schoolboy in casuals.

Stilettos, sandals,
thongs, joggers,
formal blacks and sockless.
Suits and suits
and frocks and frocks.

Phones, earplugs.
Fixed stares everywhere.
Crunch of brakes.
Tough, focused, heading
somewhere.
Not a no through road,
but home.

A homeless man
lying on a bench
in Gilbert Place.
No home to go to,
just a No Through Road.

Martin Christmas

Chance Encounter, Wakefield Street

A haibun is a Japanese form of poetic prose in which haiku move a concept forward

I first saw them in the distance over a wide Adelaide street. A tall, well-built man, walking a tiny dog – a Chihuahua, I suppose, on an extendable lead. The little creature was pure white, trotting along at a pace to match the man's, who seemed uninterested when it stopped to poke around at the base of trees for the smells that fascinate dogs. At last I spotted a car park for my hospital visit and forgot the pair until I came back to the car an hour later.

> some moments sink deep
> in preoccupied minds
> when we least expect to notice

There they were, this time coming towards me on the same footpath. 'Hello,' said the stranger. I think he spotted my clergy collar.

'What a tiny dog,' I remarked, feeling him stop, and almost loom over me, a really large figure, gentle and somehow interested.

'She's a rescue dog,' he volunteered. 'Her owners had mental health problems and I think she was badly treated. She keeps me alive, every day,' he added, to my surprise.

'What's her name?' I asked, not quick enough to judge whether he wanted me to know more of why he needed his little lifesaver.

'When I got her it was Bear.'

'Baby bear,' I muttered, amused, and at the same moment he said, 'So I call her Babe.'

> thinking we rescue
> an unwanted animal
> often the role is reversed

The little dog wagged her pretty plume of a tail on hearing her name.

'Does she feel the cold in this weather?' I wondered aloud. I expected him to say that she had a warm coat at home.

'She snuggles,' he said. 'She mostly sits on my shoulder and snuggles in.' Off he went with a 'Bye.'

'Goodbye.' I would love to know more stories of tiny Babe and the big man she rescues every day.

Dawn Colsey

I meet with a yubba in an old second-hand bookshop at Grote Street

Friday 20th, this month of autumn in my city, after work,
Instead of going to the pub I went to a second-hand
    bookshop in Grote Street.
In the quiet, I sweated and watched the sunset forgetful of
    other tasks.
Near the end of my search I thought I saw from a lot of
    books on the shelf
Books that were marked as Aboriginal.
Yoogum Yoogum, by Lionel Fogarty, Penguin Books. 1982.

I leafed through the pages of each poem quickly
I saw names, verses and time, September 1982.
Words came to my eyes as if I was walking through a long
    tunnel.
With my heart wounded I flew back to that year in one of
    the pages:
Yoogum.

I read the deep anger and hurt of many generations of totally
    oppressed Black Australians, said Gary Foley.

With those words, I landed on the roof of my old home.
It was a raid on every house in the city by the secret police.
I was already a poet with a bunch of poems surviving
the fire of oppression and many books were buried
in a huge hole on the patio.
Before I came back from my trip to USSR, 1982.

Yoogum
I read the poem, by Lionel.
I am tired of writing.
Where I can hear his rhythm of freedom
Painless are my words.

July 1982 had my own wounds and resistance lines.
Barricades incomplete, political dreams underground.
Taking hours off a duty to continue fighting until victory.

Yoogum Yoogum
Books that were buried years as seed resistance
Poetry is a flag rising upwind of freedom in people's hearts.
Poems the pathway of freedom fighters: Lionel Fogarty and
    Samuel Lafferte.

Yoogum Yoogum
Hasta la Victoria Siempre
Yubba poet

Juan Garrido Salgado

On the Fringe

Cross Rundle Street at the lights,
North down Frome
Left or right
Both familiar
Both versions of coming home.

Left: to the lower levels of a cavern that opens out and folds in.
Right: to half-made bridges and make-believe hills to die on.

This city comes alive in March,
Buskers in the mall
North or south
Both bursting
Both versions of coming home.

North: North Terrace lit up and glowing blue. Flashing
    neons and crafting shadows.
South: on and off the tram line. Slipping into pop-up venues
    and unknown shows.

This thirty-minute city
This festival state
Loved and hated
Both true
Both versions of coming home.

Alysha Herrmann

Red Salvias

Beneath the War Memorial shrine
the square patch of ground
has been planted out with red salvias

probably on purpose

now like crimson candles
they swarm beneath the edifice
of bronze and stone

and monstrous sword
that plunges at the earth
from angel hands
above a soldier
pulled from his death in mud and mire

a soul into the 'everlasting arms'

with place names embossed
around an inner vault
in lists of glorious dead
and studied shame
Gallipoli, Ypres, Passchendaele,
The Somme, Messines, Hindenburg Line…

quiet in these midwinter lunch hours
clean and quiet

and outside
beneath the War Memorial shrine
the carefully tended garden
a square patch of ground
planted out with red salvias

a profusion of terrible beauty
bleeding with an unstaunched fury

smoking
into the dark cold sky
of afternoon.

Jeff Guess

War Memorial, North Terrace, c. 1936
(State Library of South Australia, B25584)

The Tauondi Trail

after Mary Oliver's 'The Journey'

I wake. It's late enough.
I know all of a sudden –

It comes whispering under my skin, in mumbling under my
    tongue
Swoops in sideways like a lorikeet at an odd angle
Startles like electric fish netted from trawling of cinnabar dreams

In my marrow this morning, the knowing:
I must walk so as not to die.

I begin: the Torrens trail as I hear a siren singing somewhere
    past the weir.

Remnants of life scatter in my wake –
    last gasp muddy fish, tinnies, woollen hat, fast food wraps,
    Adidas athletes, t'ai chi try hards,
    iPod pedestrians, Santos students.
Each breath beats –
    to mourning howls of lion kings
    melancholic melee of godlike monkeys
    woeful blinking of soulful giraffes.
Each step brings –
rotten branches down
bluestone wall fissures whose foundations already shake
skinks to light from the rapier cracking of concrete conventions.

And then – here – a different light reveals itself!
    In river fountain's rainbow mist
    in eucalypts' leafy sun-dragons
    in sun white cockatoos picking out the gold nuggets of
    autumn.

My heart is in hands
mind in nascent wings
legs heavy and tired, about to drop off.

And then – hear – a new song of different frequency to the
    ordinary world!
    Playing amongst feathered boa of river-banked pampas,
    in windy bellows of black swans' wings
    in choral colonies of cicadas.
With this new song I walk to this different light.
    Not away from this world
    Deep, deeper, deepening to within
    where unfurling of my wings begin.

Michele Saint Yves

Tauondi is a word of the Kaurna (indigenous people of the Adelaide
Plains) akin to the English meaning of 'breakthrough'.

Elizabeth Woolcock's plea from Adelaide Gaol

Elizabeth Woolcock was hanged in Adelaide Gaol at 8 a.m. on 30
December 1873

Many's the time I tried to leave
my brandy-breath'd husband
and foul-temper'd he'd fetch me back.
I tried to please him
but he'd torment me more.
So scared I was of his meaty fists
I wanted to leave my body
with morphia I had
for sadness and sleeplessness
but they would not let me go.

I was a good wife.
When he was ill
I turned him to prevent bedsores
fed him soup
fetched a doctor to see him.
When the drug-befuddled Dr Bull
gave him mercury that made him sicker
I brought other doctors
but we ran out of money
so my brutal husband died
and like a pack of wolves
everyone turned on me
accused me of murder
and a jury took twenty minutes
to find me guilty
but what had I to gain
him dead
me homeless.

In the end
the hangman's noose
swopped one gaol for another.
Now I'm trapped here
between
my wrongful sentence
and the confessional letter
I wrote to impress the priest
who said I'd be washed white
in the precious blood of Jesus.
May he know
what I know now.
There's no washing here
just the red and the black and the pain
of in-between
of needing release
of needing to rest in rightful peace.

I slip twixt cell and slat
brick and beam
hunting for a way out
and that rustle of leaves
that close-door click
that warm breath on your cheek
is me
and all I have to say is
I beg your pardon
I beg your pardon
I beg your pardon
and thank you for the flowers

Jennifer Liston

Jacaranda in Archer Street, North Adelaide, 8 February 1954
(State Library of South Australia, B13121])

Jacarandas in North Adelaide

each November
your flowers trumpet
their arrival
in silence

you are mostly found
on the best dressed streets
wearing mauve-blue kimonos
as melodramatic
as ageing drag queens
like Narcissus you spend your days
gazing at your shadow

when the wind sits quietly
amongst branches
when the air has been picked clean of sound
we can almost hear
your faint Brazilian accents
as you talk amongst yourselves

your fingertips have smeared
purple nail polish
all over the sky
you stretch out
your long-manicured limbs
onto shelves of air
and wait for your photos to be taken

yet without your seasonal wardrobe
you find it hard to comprehend
that you are just another   tree

Jules Leigh Koch

In Passing

North Adelaide

So let me take you to this wall
where layers of plaster in odd foxy colours
fall piecemeal or fret, shearing off
in ragged fragments to leave
small red bricks exposed
or chunks of ancient river stone.
Sand's falling out like lifeblood there.

Beyond, a fine nineteenth-century home
whose back staircase climbs in weathered wood.
An antique clothes line sags across the yard;
pressed into a corner,
an ivy-covered lean-to shed.
And almost hidden, the ancient almond tree
whose drifting blossom explains
the elusive perfume in the air.
Those soft sounds you hear let you know
that chooks are in the garden, wandering free.

All at once the years compress –
as they had in colonial times
Adelaide rosellas rise, one after another,
festoons of colour flashing overhead.
There's a racket of traffic not far away
yet today in the shadow of this wall
you can picture a woman with a parasol,
children running with hoop and ball.
Or marching past, some redcoats
led by fife and drum.
Can you hear, perhaps even see
a horse and cart come down the street?

Elaine Barker

134 Jeffcott Street

My mother…
she had this small wooden jewellery box –
the kind where the lid is flanked by wooden panels
with a lid that lifts to a dancer's twirl.
But this many years after her death
the ballerina swirls and whirls to the blissful sound of silence.
In this compact chest holding all of my mother's treasures.
There's this brown button
it's kind of thick and chunky,
it's round and has four little wool holes.
The edges are scratched and rough where they were once smooth.
When I close my eyes I imagine my mother,
wrapped in a coffee-coloured cardigan.
I imagine her tucking it against her waist
and folding it across her chest,
shielding her from the day's breeze.
I imagine her rubbing her hand along the fibres of the knit,
tracing her long thin fingers down the seam,
absently fingering the buttons.
As she cycles her finger and thumb across the centre button,
I imagine it coming away.
She'd smile, and her hair would fall in her eyes,
she'd fumble the button free from the drift of wool and
walk from the window where she was catching the sun's rays
to her dressing table, and place the button in her little
    treasure chest.
She'd nestle it carefully on the orange felt right next to the
    blue braid.

The ribbon is long, and all coiled up –
it's an azure blue,
dotted with red flowers and their sunny yellow centres,
cute green leaves joining them all into a quaint little daisy chain.
This remnant is all that remains of the spool
she used to cuff her wide flared denim jeans.
In more carefree days, she'd rest her feet upon the stool
and those bell-bottomed cuffs would fold against her slender
    ankles,
she'd lean back into the cane chair,
one hand resting upon her stomach
gliding her fingers across the cheesecloth shirt.
She'd glance out across the street
from her perfect spot under the two-storeyed veranda –
the street lined with an avenue of trees –
stone pines, tall and deep, dark, emerald green on top
(my favourite colour)
And on the other end, sugar gums and river reds –
the majestic arbour with its cream-coloured bark
and patches of yellow, pink and brown,
lance shaped leaves, long and wide
spattered with life giving veins.
I imagine her favourite time was to walk
beneath the great gums during the summer time,
looking up towards the sky, blue piercing through the tree's
    canopy –
a world in a keyhole of branches,
decorated sweetly with teeny, tiny white flowers
disposed in their many panicles.

There'd be low rumblings and the chugging of cars
moving up and down the street,
and parrots flitting playfully amongst the foliage.
Sometimes,
and only sometimes,
particularly when the moon's blue matches my mood,
and my heart is heavy and my mind full,
I retrace her steps.
I remove my shoes and wriggle my toes into the earth –
earth that contains the ashes of all our ancestors,
where blood meets dirt,
and I walk bare foot along the length of Jeffcott Street
with the ghost of my mother beside me.
I take long measured strides,
while her small steps double to meet mine.
Together, we trail our fingers along the iron fence of every
      property
with our hands leap frogging between gate posts,
and our palms gliding along the rough stone fencing.
We totter our feet, carefully balancing along
the bulging roots of the trees bursting eruptions into the
      bitumen,
arms stretched out wide holding us steady.
My reminiscing trailings along the boulevard of trees becomes
a eulogy to much simpler times,
times where she still took breath,
and her crimson heart still beat with dreams and visions,
and guilty desires.

But now, now I am left with
stolen moments, abandoned hope, forgotten wishes,
and unfulfilled promises.
I am left only with the imaginings of 134 Jeffcott Street
and all that she was,
and all that she could have been
all held in the memory of a little brown button.

Tabitha Lean

Facing the sky

In Nantu Wama, just off Lefevre,
in the horse paddock,
there is a eucalyptus
that drags the leaves of its lower limbs on the ground,
clearing a bare circle as they oscillate in the breeze.
The circle looks like a dish,
an antenna aimed at the sky.
In the tree between wide-spaced branches
an orb-weaver has spun concentric circles
on silken radii as strong as steel.
This dish points low, towards the horizon.
The antennae are receivers of signals,
tiny vibrations
from an ant, or a gnat, or a whisper,
or perhaps from a satellite or a cell-tower,
bouncing messages to me
from a daughter, a bank, a merchant,
or a request to become a friend.
The horses graze on fresh winter grass
while magpies pull bugs from moist soil,
oblivious to the vibrations, dings, and rings
seeking my attention
from the zippered pocket of my jacket.

Roger Higgins

Foy & Gibson department store premises (formerly the
Grand Central Hotel) on the corner of Rundle and Pulteney
Streets, 1924 (State Library of South Australia, B72783/3)

Time Shifts at the Old Thwaites Corner

Time shifts at the corner of Pulteney Street and Rundle Mall
I see the less desirable hallmarks of 'progress'
layered over memories of amazing architecture
buildings long demolished
preserved only in archival photographs.

The old Thwaites building
now gutted and boarded up
with bland panels advertising Fringe shows
concealing its stripped interior.

Familiarity skews my vision,
overlays a 70s scene, I feel I could walk right in,
wave hello to Mr Thwaites,
Mr Lukehurst, Mr Wilson
climb the wooden staircase to my father's old grotto
where he worked for many years
pressing suits and shirts for display.

Peering out through upstairs windows
to the old ETSA building on Pulteney Street
craning to see the pageant's approach
the colourful troops and glittering floats?

This corner reinvents itself again and again.
Once there was a high-class boarding house
on the opposite side of the street, run by the Misses Bathgate.
Later, on the same site, were two hotels.

First the York, which stood for less than twenty years.
Then the Grand Central, where young Otto
the cook, only twenty-four, put his head through a broken pane
to see the lift rising to the fourth floor,
only to be struck by its descending –
the year *Titanic* sailed and sank,
and headlines declared tragedies.

I didn't know of Otto then,
as I watched John Martin's Christmas Pageant
from the old sash window above the street
but sensed the cities' ghosts, from times when such traditions
had not yet been conceived
when Otto started work in the Grand Central's kitchen,
two months before his death.

Perhaps he strolled or cycled past
the former J.T. Fitch building
on his daily route to and from work.

Who knows what the next iteration will bring.
Perhaps a mirror to the multi-storey car park
above Hungry Jacks, with exposed steel framework
and angled panels positioned to reflect laser light
postmodern ultraviolet dissolving sepia.

The fine facades of old buildings
are long demolished, and ruinous time rolls on
as Thwaites corner fades into the city archives
and young Otto rests in the cemetery at West Terrace
with a host of buried dreams.

Rest in peace, Otto,
rest in peace.

Deb Stewart

Under Adelaide Bridge

Down here
under the bridge
the night beams
a modern political rainbow of peace with globes
that glowed when Dunstan was a boy
a raven perches, watches, remembers
the dreaming of ancient hearts
the visions of new comers
protects those who travel
above, beneath, forward, back
from the distant past
into the future
beyond light

Pam Makin

Acknowledgements

Ades, David. 'Room 6, Brookman Ward', *Mapping the World*, 2008; 'Cold Front' *tamba # 36*, June 2005.

Aquilina, Jude. 'Adelaide 1970s', *On a Moon Spiced Night*, 2004; 'Early morning Bruegel', *Small City Tales of Strangeness and Beauty*, 2009.

Barker, Elaine. 'On the Torrens', *Canberra Times*, 1991, *Friendly Street Poetry Reader* No. 16, 1992; 'In passing' and 'Sandalwood', *The Day Lit by Memory,* 2008; 'The Turban', *My Feathered Fingers,* 2019.

Christmas, Martin. 'CBD Reality', *Random Adventures*, 2019; '10:31', *The Deeper Inner*, 2018, 'No Through Road' *StepAway Magazine,* UK online journal, 2017.

Costello, Moya. 'Adelaide, South Australia', *Friendly Street Poetry Reader* No. 16, 1992, *Small Ecstasies*, 1994.

Flett, Alison. 'Adelaide I dream you', *Westerly Magazine*, October 2018, *Australian Poetry Journal Anthology*, 2019.

Foulkes, Sharon. 'The Walk on by Blues', *New Poets 20*, 2019.

Garrido-Salgado, Juan. 'I meet with a yubba in an old second-hand bookshop at Grote Street', *Hope Blossoming in Their Ink*, 2020.

Gower, Jill. 'Resilience', *South East City Stories,* March 2012.

Guess, Jeff. 'Balls', *Friendly Street Poetry Reader* #15, 1991; 'The Egyptian Room', *Leaving Maps*, 1984; 'Field of Dreams' *Weekend Plus*, 10 April 2014; 'Adelaide', *Replacing Fuses in the House of Cards,* 1988; 'Frog Cakes', *Living in the Shade of Nothing Solid*, 1998; 'Red Salvias' and 'City Street Sweeper', *Rites of Arrival: Poems from Museums of the History Trust of SA*,

1990; '*Popeye*' and others in *Dream Houses – Adelaide in Poems and Pictures* exhibition at David Jones in Adelaide, 1990.

Higgins, Roger. 'Living Underwater during Drought', *Surf Sounds*, 2014; 'State Library Mortlock Wing', *New Poets 13*, 2008; 'Facing the Sky', *Facing the Sky,* Ginninderra Press.

Koch, Jules Leigh. 'Jacarandas in North Adelaide', originally published under the title 'Jacarandas' in *Friendly Street Reader* No. 42, *Dream Water Fragment*, 2017.

Spencer, Beth. 'This Girl is Missing' is drawn from a longer piece called 'The Mummy's Foot' which was published in *Things in a Glass Box*, 1994; it also won the Age Short Story award and was broadcast on ABC *Poetica*.

Stewart, Deb. 'The Weir – Changing' and 'Beatlemania' from the verse novel manuscript *An Adelaide Boy* and 'The Weir – Changing', *The White Line of Language*, 2019.

Sullivan, Thom. 'Adelaide', *Westerly Special Online Issue*, No. 6 September 2018.

Taylor, Andrew. 'The Adelaide Gaol Seen from the Golf Course', *The Friendly Street Poetry Reader*, 1977.

Tipping, Richard. 'Adelayed Reaction', *Tommy Ruff: Adelaide Poems,* 2014, *Friendly Street Poets 39: Silver Singing Streams,* 2015.

Walker, Amelia. 'Him' and 'Pancake Kitchen, Gilbert Place', *Fat Streets & Lots of Squares,* 2003.

www.ingramcontent.com/pod-product-compliance
Lightning Source LLC
Chambersburg PA
CBHW071845080526
44589CB00012B/1113